What peopl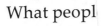

Presen

The crises we are in are the result of thousands of years of the systematisation of a lack of presence in our culture, institutions and economics. Grounding our activism in presence feels essential to me, thank you Lynne for providing us with this helpful guide.

Dr Gail Bradbrook, co-founder, Extinction Rebellion

Presence Activism provides a hard-hitting overview of the polycrises that humanity is facing while providing a path to move beyond climate anxiety and despair toward skilful action grounded in Presence. Lynne shares practices and insights drawn from her front-line experience as an activist in the field, spiritual teacher and leader of community groups. She shares her own personal story and journey from an activism driven by anxiety and frustration resulting in burnout and despair, to one of effectiveness, ease and renewed energy. Her models of the Presence Flower and the Anxiety Flower provide a non-linear guide on where we can take action, dissolve our barriers and attend to the challenges of the future by coming from the best possible place — the 'here and no.' An indispensable book for all change-agents.

Steven D'Souza, Senior Client Partner, Korn Ferry, author of the *Not Knowing* trilogy

A masterpiece! Lynne's profound wisdom, lived experience, academic research and her compelling Presence Flower will inspire you to take action for a sustainable future, while preserving your well-being. Lynne offers a refreshing approach to activism and calls us to action in a viable way. She supports us to navigate the challenges of overwhelm, despair and hopelessness through a deep sense of connection, direct awareness and compassion. She invites us to be fully present, embrace the actuality of the now and refuse to look away from the pressing challenges of our time. This book is testament to the light of Lynne's soul, heart and life-force, her profound understanding of the human experience and her unwavering commitment to earth and human survival. I wholeheartedly recommend it for those willing to take the transformative journey towards a future where embodying presence and activism go hand in hand as a force for positive change.

Kay Louise Aldred, author of *Mentorship with Goddess*, *Making Love with the Divine*, and *Somatic Shamanism*; co-author of *Embodied Education*

This book does three things particularly well. It serves as a guide to the inner attentiveness that each of us must hold to if we are to recognise and respond in a reasonable way to multiple crises and anxieties. It links together many recent and contemporary writings on presence, activism and climate anxiety with sympathetic readings that emphasise their meaning for the heart as much as the mind. It has an immediacy that appeals directly to the intuition, 'calling' directly to those attuned to its message. This enlivening book is an enjoyable read and will also be helpful for those on other paths of climate, social and ecological activism. It contributes to both a vibrant contemporary feminism, and the resurgence of modern stoicism.

Jonathan Gosling, Emeritus Professor of Leadership, University of Exeter, Principal Consultant, Pelumbra

This is a deeply insightful, practical and compassionate book on how we can adapt, cope & move humanity during this urgent climate crisis. Lynne's writing and research is extremely thorough yet accessible, and the topic she addresses can help all concerned souls to experience presence without feeling depressed or helpless. It is a profound spiritual call to action with kindness and hope. This book is very useful for activists, teachers, scholars and students looking to restore their inner courage and optimism in spite of the challenges. Read, reflect and experience.

Professor Atul K. Shah, City, University of London, author of *Inclusive and Sustainable Finance*

We have to be present in order to make change, and that is a skill. In addition, in our current context, honesty, empathy and compassion have become survival skills. We need to hone these skills, and to do so in times of breaking will require enormous strength and courage. In other words, we have our work cut out, this book helps us to reflect on the urgent question of how to go forward.

Claire Farrell, co-founder, Extinction Rebellion

Lynne has skilfully applied the ancient spiritual practice of presence to help activists and others cope with overwhelming feelings around climate and ecological crisis. Climate grief and anxiety has become a major issue, especially among young people. She explains at length, how anxiety affects both body and psyche, resulting in overwhelm and burnout. Her interpretation of different aspects of presence, offers practical steps to enable others to connect with their spiritual core. This can restore balance, strength and clarity in choice of actions. Similar to the martial arts practice of non-attachment and non-doing, presence allows the right move to spring from an impartial awareness. She explores different activist movements and their approaches to change. She has researched and offers a range of sources to back her approach. An empowering and useful book.

Rachael Clyne, psychotherapist, poet and author of *Singing at the Bone Tree*, *Girl Golem*, and *You'll Never Be Anyone Else*

Passionate, engaged, idealistic and emotionally intelligent, Lynne Sedgmore's *Presence Activism* inspires and gives profoundly practical advice. With a background in high profile mainstream leadership and feminist spirituality, Lynne absolutely understands humanity's predicament and the mix of activism and deep personal change needed to transform and heal the global crisis, and move towards sustainability, social justice and a renewed appreciation of our beautiful planet
William Bloom, author of *The Endorphin Effect* and *Psychic Protection*

Activist or not, this remarkable book asks how we can ensure our own resilience whilst facing the overwhelming anxiety of climate peril and unprecedented existential catastrophe. Through the practice of 'presence', Lynne Sedgmore offers us another way to align ourselves to the challenges of the ecological emergency; a way that respects our innate interconnection and our natural alignment to our purpose and our potential. A way that is beyond confrontation and opposition, and the metaphors of fighting and war. In a world all too full of concern and apprehension, *Presence Activism* has inspired me with hope for the future!
Jon Cousins, 'Green' Mayor of Glastonbury in 2016 and from 2021–'23

Lynne Sedgmore is a wise spirit, an elder who offers us a rare gift of practical mysticism in order that we can be activist-contemplatives, able to be present to the climate peril we face.

This book is a must read for all activists and all humans who care deeply about the planet, each other and their own well-being.
Dr Simon Western, Chief Executive, Eco-Leadership Institute

Many activists are spiritually driven so when things don't improve, or even worsen, they may suffer deep anxiety and trauma. Lynne Sedgmore's book *Presence Activism: A Profound Antidote to Climate Anxiety* examines how we may become unbalanced and close down to protect our core essence. Using beautiful mandalas of Presence and Anxiety Flowers Lynne lays out various facets of portals, energies, essences, gnosis and self. She examines how anxiety unfolds and its triggers, alongside providing a process to reconcile spiritual, mental, emotional, and physical realities. Through sharing her own life journey with key insights and lessons learned, she demonstrates how Presence guides and illuminates us through Shadow into Light. We see how to lead and inspire others as we face the greatest peril humanity has faced by stepping into Presence.

Dr Michael White, ocean and climate scientist, author of *The Sea Turtles of Rakahanga and Tongareva*, President of Hakono Hararanga Tongareva Atoll

Group Relations, psychoanalysis and ancient spiritual wisdoms are entwined in this labyrinthine book. Lynne takes us into the foundations of our current situation of "Climate Peril," fearlessly looking into our potential extinction, then embracing it with both assured unknowing, and unshaken noetic knowing. This is a guidebook to planetary relationship and human flourishing that is both self-revelatory and socially-illuminating. We have done this to ourselves, how can we live with the consequences? Presence is articulated in a way that ignites curiosity about the world and how we can live in it. Lynne's Presence Gnosis will provide many executives and leaders a frame for an awakening that can transform our social order in profound ways. The psychoanalytically informed community will find resources for activism and an openness to what is yet to emerge. If you have fallen asleep, this book is gentle reminder to awaken. A masterclass from a Living Luminary.

Dr Leslie B Brissett, Group Relations Programme Director at the Tavistock Institute of Human Relations (UK)

Some of the most violent places I've been were peace marches. Some of the most exhausting were climate change events. We so much want to affect positive change in the world. I love what Lynne is reminding us, that when we act from presence, challenges become spiritual opportunities and our actions become grounded in reality. Her book is practical and mystical, embodied and deeply interesting.

Julia Paulette Hollenbery, healer, teacher, and author of *The Healing Power of Pleasure*

We are living through a once-in-a-civilisation moment ripe for rebirth. Such a metamorphic moment invokes dissonance and anxiety, distracting us from the quality of consciousness needing to be born through our thoughts, words and deeds. Amid anxiety it's easy to succumb to the frantic patching up of symptoms unfolding from the myriad crises, overlooking the deeper underlying causes. This urgent text deals with the root problem at source, our consciousness and presence. This invigorating book aligns the inner-outer nature of our humanity. It is packed full of practical wisdom, drawing upon Lynne Sedgmore's many years of practice and encyclopaedic knowledge. Lynne is a timely wisdom-weaver who captures the practical art of cultivating the wisdom required for activating regenerative futures.

Giles Hutchins, regenerative leadership specialist, UK, author of *Leading by Nature*, *Future-Fit*, *Regenerative Leadership*, and *The Illusion of Separation*

In her illuminating book Dr. Sedgmore skilfully explores the transformative potential of embracing presence as a transformative force. She unravels the notion that presence is a potent antidote to anxiety. She also lays the vital groundwork that empowers activists to cultivate unwavering resilience amidst the perpetual flux of our world. Through the pages of this timeous and important work, Lynne's lifelong commitment to inner growth finds vivid expression. This book offers readers an invaluable roadmap to embody presence and to forge a path towards a more grounded and purposeful existence.

Elmor van Staden PhD, IT Service Delivery Executive, South Africa

In this beautiful, passionate and timely book, Lynne Sedgmore explores the deep connection between spirituality and activism. Spiritual awakening is the most urgent need of our time, and this book points the way to a harmonious future in which we may become able to live in harmony with ourselves, and with the natural world.

Steve Taylor PhD, author of *The Leap* and *DisConnected*

I sit here with a steady flow of tears for the raw beauty, truth and beautifully articulated wisdom you have expressed in *Presence Activism*. For many years I have been shedding and working with Presence, without knowing that this was what was happening to me and my service out in the world. Reading from Presence in each chapter I felt a different sense of learning, and depth of emotion. This book, your teachings, the flowers and the wisdom petals bring together a rich garden of abundance that can feed our souls, help our minds understand and soothe our breaking hearts. I know in my bones that this book will enable many therapists and healers to understand another level of anxiety and despair. Many of us are seeing so much of this right now. You give supportive meaning and a clear perspective on how to move through, how to be with, and to be present with all that is. Thank you and Blessed Be.

Angie Twydall, Founder of the Sanctuary of Sophia, Priestess and Healer

Lynne has offered the world a precious treasure through her message in this book. Her integrity and commonsense is a healing balm in the face of frequently anxiety-inducing data concerning the very real critical climate emergency that we find ourselves living through. The suggestions she makes for activists, and those held in a space of distress or grief around our changing ecosystem, are simple and rooted in a deeply considered and heartfelt space of compassionate witnessing that Lynne so deeply embodies through her work, teachings and publications. I feel blessed through every encounter with her as an author, fellow priestess, and lifelong mentor and living example of change making for the good of all.

Bliss Magdalena Qadesh, Founder of Stroud Goddess Temple and PhD Researcher, Centre for Gender and Violence Research, University of Bristol

We are in climate peril, and time is not on our side. *Presence Activism* is the book we all need right now, in this present moment. Lynne Sedgmore herself walks the delicate balance of powerful mystic, with her rich and depth-filled presence wisdom that edges up with her fierce, informed activist warrior, dramatically mirroring both the poignantly regenerative and the ragingly ferocious edges of Mother Earth right now. Rich with resources to motivate and mobilise the reader, Lynne gives us a map (a high-octane GPS!) to deepen and expand our presence to move beyond our overwhelming anxiety and crippling fear; into activating our courage, putting the climate and ecological crisis on everyone's lips, and to taking action. Both a clarion call and a prayerful practice, *Presence Activism* supports all of us in our greater understanding of our interconnectedness with All beings, and how to move the Kincentric mindset out into doing the work of rebalancing life on Mother Earth.

Sandra Bargman, author, inter-spiritual minister, actor, climate-reality leader, podcast host of *The Edge of Everyday*

Presence Activism

A Profound Antidote to Climate Anxiety

Presence Activism

A Profound Antidote to Climate Anxiety

Lynne Sedgmore

CHANGEMAKERS
BOOKS

London, UK
Washington, DC, USA

CollectiveInk

First published by Changemakers Books, 2024
Changemakers Books is an imprint of Collective Ink Ltd.,
Unit 11, Shepperton House, 89 Shepperton Road, London, N1 3DF
office@collectiveinkbooks.com
www.collectiveinkbooks.com
www.changemakers-books.com

For distributor details and how to order please visit the 'Ordering' section on our website.

ISBN: 978 1 80341 602 1
978 1 80341 617 5 (ebook)
Library of Congress Control Number: 2023941815

A CIP catalogue record for this book is available from the British Library.

Design: Lapiz Digital Services

UK: Printed and bound by CPI Group (UK) Ltd, Croydon, CR0 4YY
Printed in North America by CPI GPS partners

We operate a distinctive and ethical publishing philosophy in
all areas of our business, from our global network of authors to
production and worldwide distribution.

Contents

"*Ask anyone who's nearly died, you should live in the moment.*"
Jodi Picoult

"*On the last day of the world, I would want to plant a tree.*"
W.S. Merwin

In deep gratitude to my granddaughters, Caitlin and Sian, I learn from them every day.

To Luis, Brandon, Darcy, Dempsey, Josh, Ralph, Ben and Gwen my nephews and nieces.

To all young climate activists across the world, and to future generations.

To John, my husband, whose presence and unconditional love calm and light my life.

To my daughter Keri, and son-in-law Terry for their fantastic anti-HS2 activism, resilience and loving presence in my life.

To Ruth and Beth, my stepdaughters for your beautiful presence in my life.

To all the climate and feminist activists who have personally graced my life, together we do our best to make the world a better place for everyone.

To Dan, Amy and Jane, the fabulous Plotgate community farm team.

To Hameed (A. H. Almaas) whose exquisite and profound presence and teachings continually transform my life and realisations.

To all my shining Luminary students, the presence of every one of you has affected me deeply.

In memory of my ex-husband Jeff Davies who passed in March 2023, in gratitude for our love and your presence in my life.

In memory of other friends who have passed while writing this book, Barry Taylor, Jan Storey, Jennifer Sharpe, Graham Harman-Baker, and Christine Harman-Baker.

List of Figures

Forewords

By Mayor Indra Donfrancesco and
Rev. Prof. Stephen G Wright

Indra Donfrancesco

Lynne Sedgmore inspired me to read her book ... even though I have a dusty case full of unread books, from *"How to save the world"* to *"Head for the hills and grow cabbages."*

I really really needed to read this particular book.

As with most of Lynne's teaching, I was soon able to apply her wisdom practically, both as an activist and, more recently, as leader, green councillor, and Mayor of Glastonbury council.

The face of activism has changed significantly in the last thirty years. Burnout is an occupational hazard of being a good person in an unfair civilisation. It also happens in spite of, or because of, great sacrifices activists continually make. Lynne reminds us of our armour within, our inner resilience. She also illustrates that, with practice, we are impenetrable, always are, and always can be. She understands the ravages of activism as well as its highs. She illuminates the importance of learning to live in these challenging times in the face of climate peril as a conscious being staying in presence. Lynne has done the work. She provides a map for others to do their own work, if they so choose.

Most of all, this book creates space to find and welcome our courage, beyond anxiety. It offers a clear pathway and process to "bring about profound change through being fully present within the realities of climate peril," beyond burnout.

The unique tips, insights and practices are a visual deep dive with quotes and useful analysis calling upon favourite writers from Lynne's extensive library. She shares her visceral experiences of presence throughout her life, wisdom from other teachers and her thirst for crossing new boundaries and thresholds.

As activists, we are constantly replaying the old fight against a status quo, alongside knowing that something "new" is happening and needs to emerge. Lynne is offering us next-level activism, an activism steeped in trust, love, joy, peace, and being in full control: being the dance.

Indra Donfrancesco, veteran activist of thirty years, present Mayor of Glastonbury town

Rev. Prof. Stephen G Wright

'Tipping point' is a familiar concept applied to the climate crisis engulfing our planet. Less often do we see it referred to in the context of our way of being as humans. Lynne, in her inimitable and forthright style, pulls no punches in summarising how the earth is in crisis and also what it is to be human.

Across the globe many are responding to that challenge, not just to address and mitigate the worst effects of the climate catastrophe and all that follows in its trail — the collapse of ecological, political, economic and social systems — but also to help people. Help us to avoid the likelihood of a decline into the worst and most brutal aspects of our behaviour when frightened. Help us to transform consciousness so that whatever emerges from the collapse, and remember this is a gradual, accelerating process not an event, might yet offer new ways of being together and at-one with all of life.

Lynne contributes to that global movement by not only pointing towards the problems, but also showing ways, in the development of her model of Presence, a passage through.

Whatever your belief system, massive shifts are under way in the material and non-material realms. Mother Earth, in pain, is forcing a rethink of our separation from her. A new age in that sense really is upon us and is unstoppable. No matter what theories or theologies we cling to, the status quo simply is no longer an option. This, astrologically, is the age of Aquarius;

characterised by a rebalancing of the masculine and feminine, models of cooperation and collaboration to get things done, a restoration of respect and reverence of nature, reconnecting to all-that-is while rejecting separation, manifesting in a thousand ways from the ecology movements to the renewal of goddess worship, from the feminist and other liberation movements to the worship of nature. Lynne illuminates these many strands and weaves them into the foundation of, and a summons to, Presence.

I first came across the notion of 'presencing' long ago in my early professional nursing days. It was an encouragement in the education of nurses to be more connected, more individualised in their approach to patients at a time when nursing was seen to be becoming technically rich but spiritually poor. Drawing on ancient Eastern philosophies and the often unacknowledged Western traditions of 'coming alongside' in service or the pre-Christian notions of oneness with all of life. My own great Teacher Ram Dass was one of the earliest to coin the phrase 'Be Here Now' in his seminal 60's 'bible,' *Be Here Now.*

We see echoes of Presence in the interconnectedness of quantum physics, in the contemplative tradition of unity consciousness, in the work of modern writers urging interspirituality, holism, interbeing or the many variations of the perennial philosophy.

Lynne acknowledges a long train of influences and ancestry in her work; we have a good view because we stand on giants' shoulders. And yet, as inspirational poet Eliot (his works loved by Lynne and myself) reminds us, 'we cannot dance to an antique drum' — each age, each generation must reinterpret and co-create truth for its own time and circumstances.

As feminist and lesbian poet Audre Lorde suggests, 'the master's tools will never dismantle the master's house.' The new tools that Lynne offers us, are needed to build the new way of being. Hope, as Lynne explores, is not about creating trust in an illusory future. It is about learning to live fully and together in unity conscious in the here and now. That is Presence, both individual and collective. Rising to face what is and working to cocreate what might be.

Activism without Presence is carnage. Unless we have clarity of intention, unless we have 'done the work' on our inner selves to release us from our ego agendas, we will simply re-inflict the wounds of the past. No small task. Lynne's vision of Presence as concept and action, stirs us to recognise that outer change is corrupted unless inner change precedes it. Presence offers us a toolkit for such inner-outer transformation.

As I have explored in my own related book on this theme (*Fugue*), what we have to address is the Cause of the causes — the deep-rooted alienation of a great mass of human beings, for all kinds of reasons, from connectedness to all of life, reverence for it, for respect for our place in it in the great chain of being. When we appreciate the enormity and glory of All-that-is, how could we not be brought to humility and Presence in the face of it? How could we not cherish and appreciate it? Presence draws this out of us, and into service.

What shines through in Lynne's work is the interweaving of the personal and transpersonal, the unification of the one in the many. If there is not 'one size fits all' in the enormity of what we face, works like Lynne's are a facet carved in a ballroom mirror. No one reflects the whole, but gathered they offer different perspectives, different options, the genesis of a new whole that is more than, other than, the sum of its parts. Presence offers us one more facet to reflect and bring light to that new wholeness. This Presence is not passive, it does not buy into the misunderstanding of the contemplative, the reflective, as a spiritually navel-gazing person in escape from the suffering of the world. Lynne's approach to Presence is active, it is action orientated, it is a deep dive inward in order to surface and serve outward. It is an engaged spirituality needed now in these times more than ever.

For these times are not like before. There have been moments in history when humanity created disaster. The slow accretion of human planetary activity has brought us to the brink of destruction; it's now under way. The bomb has been dropped. It's not a big one-off blast. It is slow, accumulative and unstoppable, and we are going to have to learn to live with it.

To live with and beyond it we will need Presence in all its forms across place and time.

Our technology is not going to save us. Only a profound, inner shift of consciousness, a deep and global emergence of Presence, an opening of the heart to compassion, is going to save us. It will be a damn close-run thing. This work, Lynne's work, is soul food for such a time.

Rev. Prof. Stephen G Wright, spiritual director at the Sacred Space Foundation, teacher of the *Heartfullness* contemplative-mystics programme, author of *Burnout: A Spiritual Crisis; Coming Home; Contemplation and Heartfullness; Fugue: Climate Crisis and Collapse — a Spiritual Response*

Acknowledgements

I thank everyone who has contributed, supported and encouraged me throughout my life.

My presence work and practices have emerged from a lifetime of learning from others who have travelled this journey both before, and alongside me. I thank all those who were part of supporting my leadership presence in the world of further education for many years. Thank you to all the feminist and climate activists who have inspired me and worked alongside me. I am grateful to all of you, too many to name. You know who you are.

I thank all those I have journeyed with in Extinction Rebellion, the Glastonbury Town Deal and the spiritual communities of Ridhwan UK3, One Spirit UK, Buddhist, Christian, Interfaith, Goddess and Glastonbury I have belonged to.

This book would not have manifested without the support and influence of some wonderful people I must name. My presence teachers include Hameed, Miranda, Russ Hudson, Don Riso, Sandy, Tejo, Joyce, Prakash Michael, and all my Luminary students.

The exquisite and profound teachings and books of A. H. Almaas (Hameed) on presence deserve a special mention. His effect on me has been powerful and liberating, beyond words.

I am grateful for the many years of spiritual support, wisdom and friendship of Stephen Wright, Atul Shah, Simon Western, Dame Ann Limb, Jon Cousins, Indra Donfrancesco, Lynne Foote, Jan Storey, Bawa Jain, Barry Taylor, Elisabeth Tham, Peter Hawkins and Josie Luton; your presence has enriched my life. Thank you, June Boyce-Tillman, for your wisdom and guidance through my Doctoral work on presence.

I am indebted to Tim Ward for his belief in my book, plus his wisdom and professional expertise, as well as his perceptive insight and our spiritual connection.

Words cannot express my love for and gratitude to Stephen Wright and Indra Donfrancesco for writing such thoughtful forewords.

I couldn't have completed the book without my fellow presence companion and beloved husband, John Capper, who constantly supports and nourishes my presence, heart, spirit and creativity.

I am blessed and grateful to have an expert and creative designer, Richard Kingston, who translated my thoughts into beautiful models and also finalised the technical details of the manuscript.

Thank you to everyone who wrote an endorsement; I greatly appreciate your time and affirmation.

And finally, thank you to the team at Changemakers and Collective Ink for all your guidance and support in manifesting this book.

I am grateful to you all.

Introduction

"Your true home is in the here and the now." **Thich Nhat Hanh**

Too many activists that I meet and with whom I protest are exhausted, weary and burnt out, despite their incredible commitment, urgency and passion for saving our planet. The relentless opposition, denial, blocking and wilful inaction of governments and corporates can feel like banging your head against a steel wall. Climate activists are working incredibly hard to ensure the resilience of our planet. An important question is, How do they ensure their own resilience?

My aim in writing this book is to support activists to develop their innate capacity to cope and to act effectively amidst the challenges, complexities, anxiety, stress and existential threat of living in the face of climate peril. Activism steeped in fear and anxiety can lead to skepticism, burnout, catastrophism and an endless supply of causes to fight.

Presence Activism: A Profound Solution to Climate Anxiety integrates presence into activism through a clear process that alleviates climate anxiety, nourishes activists, and fosters healthy relationships and right action. An activism that feels effortless and flows in alignment with our own unique purpose and role in the saving of our planet. A resilient activism no longer steeped in the illusion of separation, but informed by the visceral knowing of presence, interconnection, different senses of self, and views of reality. An activism beyond metaphors of fighting and war.

The Presence Flower is a profound approach of seeing, owning and allowing all aspects of anxiety until we can ultimately relax and dissolve those parts that get triggered and stimulated by climate peril. Presence is an anxiety antidote.

I began therapy in my twenties, I have been peer counseled, I had a coach, a mentor, a spiritual director, and I have consistently undertaken inner formation and development to understand and deconstruct my personality. Alongside these, I have practiced presence. Without a doubt, the most powerful and profound ways in which I have moved through my own anxiety are through the potency of presence.

Climate Peril

Climate change is a term that I find too gentle. I prefer the terms climate crisis, climate risk, climate emergency, climate catastrophe, climate breakdown or climate peril. I use the term climate peril throughout to emphasise how urgent and imperative the current situation is. Much has been written on climate change, so in Chapter 1 I provide an overview of climate peril and the three different responses of mitigation and adaptation, deep adaptation and extinction. I also explore hope, ways of reclaiming hope and coping with, or without, a sense of hope.

Climate peril involves environmental degradation, global warming and the possibility of extinction. We are living in an unprecedented time of depletion and destruction of our planet. The dire climate and ecological problems confronting humanity are a consequence, or symptom, of the destructive ecological footprint of humanity resulting in a massive reduction or demise of many species. The survival of humanity is threatened, as we are interdependent with all living beings. Additional complications and demands on resources will be created by increases in migrations of people away from coastal flood zones, wars, famines, genocides, air pollution and natural disasters. The melting of the glaciers, including the huge ones in Greenland and Antarctica, will cause rises in global sea levels and will adversely affect coastal communities around the world.

The United Nations' Intergovernmental Panel on Climate Change (IPCC)[1] has been issuing warnings for thirty-two years and has provided six reports since its establishment in 1988. It continues to emphasise the imperative to act sooner rather than later on climate change.

In January 2023, the Secretary General of the United Nations, Antonio Guterres, gave a speech at the annual gathering of global leaders at the World Economic Forum in Davos, Switzerland. I watched his speech on BBC news coverage in which he stated firmly that, "We are flirting with climate disaster, an existential challenge. Every day brings a new climate horror that we need to face, the commitment to limit the global temperature rise to 1.5 degrees nearly going up in smoke. Without further action we are heading to a 2.8 degree increase with devastating consequences including a death sentence. All this has been clear for decades from many difficult sources. Fossil fuel enablers are still behaving irresponsibly and need to be held to account. We know the ecosystem meltdown is cold scientific fact. Things are piling up like cars in a chain reaction crash." Indeed, in May 2023, research from the World Meteorological Organisation (WMO) warned that the world is almost certain to experience new record temperatures and a 66 percent chance of crossing the 1.5 degrees target, by 2027.

How do we live, act, be effective activists and cope, in the face of all of this? When we live from presence, climate peril can be a portal to a renewed consciousness and a grounded form of activism for ourselves, others, and the planet.

Presence

To understand how and why presence is a profound antidote, in Chapter 2, I explore presence within five different domains: Personal Presence, Professional Presence, Transpersonal Presence, Nature Presence, and Being Here Now. Within each domain I provide an overview of understandings and contributions of presence, then I describe my own experience within each domain. I also describe my own experiences of the transmission of presence.

The Presence Flower is described in detail in Chapter 3. It is an unfolding process which fosters access to seven Presence Essences of resilience, peace, trust, strength, love, flow and joy. The impact of accessing one or more of these seven essences means we can be both contemplative and active, inwardly and externally focussed, calm and effective. For those of you who have not yet discovered these essences, the Presence Flower is a process for experiencing them. For those of you already familiar with essences, I integrate presence into an accessible and practical path to support anyone who cares about our climate and ecological crises, especially climate activists.

I am a presence teacher. For many years I have been saying that whatever the issue, problem or constraint the answer is presence. What I mean by this is that the more present and expanded we are in our interconnection with all beings, with nature and the universal source of life, the more we can act in ways that co-create solutions, especially ones that protect rather than harm our planet. The more our capacity to be in presence, the more we will find equanimity and skill amidst whatever is happening around us. Over the years, many of my Luminary students have told me that they feel more equipped to act, lead, and cope through learning to be more present, especially during the pandemic. They have asked me to share a more explicit version of my presence teachings. This book is my response to that request.

Presence can change or relax anything, including overwhelming anxiety and fear. It is everywhere, literally everywhere, both inside and outside of us, whether we are conscious of it or not. In presence, we are held and we feel safe, whatever the circumstances. Presence increases our capacity to cope with challenges and to act with skill in the world.

Climate Anxiety

Climate peril affects people deeply. It can feel a massive responsibility, a huge burden, yet it can also be a powerful opportunity to rethink who we are and how we choose to live. Chapter 4 dives into the nature, symptoms and scope of climate anxiety. It introduces the Anxiety Flower, the counterpart to the Presence Flower, to illustrate different types of anxiety, and how they can be dissolved by presence.

More and more people are experiencing profound uncertainty and anxiety about the state of the world, their safety and their livelihood. I no longer believe in any kind of return to what was once considered to be normality. The world has always been full of change, challenge, tragedy and uncertainty, yet climate peril is unprecedented in the challenges it brings. Global communication and social media, alongside the unrelenting news focus on negativity, can make it seem like there is only suffering, confusion, chaos and ever-increasing hardship wherever you look. Inevitably, the various events of climate peril generate significant psychological and emotional stress in all of us. Our emotions, psyches, bodies, spirits and souls may feel constantly depleted. It is easy to get off balance, to feel pulled in all directions, to feel deeply anxious and to forget what really matters to us in such a crazy, chaotic and complicated world.

Despite many existing conventional approaches to anxiety, there is a growing realisation of their limitations in addressing and solving the climate anxiety many people, young and old, are facing today. Despite the range of solutions, climate anxiety is increasing across all age groups. Without doubt, we need to develop and expand our personal internal coping mechanisms, responses and capacities. I am offering presence as a significant path to dissolving climate anxiety and developing a profound capacity to live and to act in the face of climate peril.

Presence Activism

Presence Activism is intended both for anyone new to the practice and concept of presence as well as someone already familiar with presence. It is an invitation to live and act from within the sacredness and preciousness of life. To be an activist from the direct visceral knowing of presence, being deeply present to what is emerging, and discerning how a deeper wisdom is asking us to show up, engage and act. To act in the world through an activism that feels natural, effortless, flowing in alignment with our purpose and the saving of our planet. To act for the higher good, well-being and maximum potential of everyone.

Presence Activism begins with each one of us being the most expanded we can be and from the profound understanding that our states of being, senses of self and views of reality matter as much as our actions. An activism without burnout or overwhelming anxiety, as our actions flow from a sense of being grounded, boundless, whole, interconnected and abundant.

I have developed Presence Activism from my own journey as an activist and from learning from other activists I have journeyed alongside. Chapter 5 explains Presence Activism and explores relevant climate activist movements, especially those by which I have been influenced.

I offer practical suggestions on how to embody Presence Activism in the world in Chapter 6. Presence Activism can be far-reaching in its impact as an accessible and practical path for activism when embodied in the world as service, right action and healthy relationships.

Chapter 7 is an exploration of the inner shifts and new perspectives that acting and living from presence can engender. Presence Activism is underpinned and nourished by the visceral knowing of interconnectedness with the earth and all living beings. It involves moving beyond limiting beliefs, concepts and personality constraints. It fosters an authentic, direct and visceral knowing of the innate goodness of every human being. It enables the capacity to co-create a healthy relationship with our planet as an interdependent, breathing, living, complex ecosystem of which we are an integral part.

My Intention

I want to support and liberate the lives of anyone, especially activists, who may be feeling anxious or overwhelmed, their energies dulled by living in these complex, frightening and challenging times.

Eco-, environmental and climate activists concerned with the future of the planet's environment have been protesting, informing and campaigning for many years. They are responding to numerous, life-threatening perils, alongside the threat of the end of the world as we know it. They are faced with the possibility of extinction, the resources of the planet being irretrievably depleted and social disruption on an unprecedented scale. This is something very different from what took place when I was young. When I began as an activist in the 1970s, we had hope, genuine hope that we would make the world a better place, that things would get better. Now I am sixty-seven; I could die tomorrow having lived a full life. I find it horrifying that our young people have to face the possibility of an early death linked to the death of the world. My granddaughters are seventeen and twenty, my great nephews and nieces are as young as three years old, far too young to have to look into the face of climate peril and watch the adults in power fail to tackle the most important issues facing the world today.

I admire the thousands of people I meet in Glastonbury and on Extinction Rebellion protests who have chosen to devote their time, sometimes their whole lives, to climate activism. I understand why some climate activists are willing to risk everything to work towards saving a dying planet, as they feel their very existence at risk. I have developed Presence Activism for everyone. I offer a path and process to develop an enhanced capacity to act skilfully and to be self-sustaining, resilient and successful in the face of solving climate peril and the ecological crisis. May presence be a genuine antidote to any anxiety you are experiencing.

May my book support you to be and act in your own unique way, as a Presence Activist: deeply inspired, and nourished, by presence.

Chapter 1

The Context of Climate Peril

***

"Humankind cannot bear very much reality." **T.S. Eliot**

***

Introduction

So much is written, and available, on climate change, biodiversity and the ecological crisis. There are many different and conflicting views to consider—so much scientific and technical data. At times I have felt lost in the mass of information available and the opposing views, yet I kept going with the support and insight of my husband, friends and fellow activists.

In this contextual chapter, I share my explorations, traversing and understanding of climate peril through the three lenses of mitigation and adaptation, deep adaptation and extinction. I include the thoughts, views and influences of key writers who have shaped my view on the many climate and ecological problems confronting humanity.

I conclude this chapter by sharing my own viewpoint. I don't expect or want you to agree with me; this is not a polemic. My aim is to assist you in your own understanding and to inform you in your own insights and viewpoints as an underpinning to your climate activism.

The Peril

What are climate activists facing? A climate peril caused by human activities such as burning fossil fuels, deforestation and industrial agriculture. These activities are leading to rising temperatures, extreme weather events and rising sea levels. We now live in the Anthropocene Age, a geological age marked by the ways in which human beings have negatively and irrevocably affected the climate and their environment.

Climate change and the ecological crisis form a large and complex field on which much has been written. Mark Maslin in *How to Save Our Planet: The Facts* (2021), provides invaluable facts and figures to understand the urgency and the need to act immediately.

Our planet and its atmosphere is a complex, living system whose future is dependent on every living and non-living subsystem. Some argue that the biggest threat to continued life on earth for every species is not fossil fuel emissions but the loss of forests, soil, wetlands, and marine ecosystems. When the natural, breathing, living, interdependent ecosystem of organic relationships break down, the results are global warming or global cooling spinning out of control. The ecological and climate crises we face are multifactorial and nonlinear.

On May 17th, 2023, research from the World Meteorological Organisation (WMO) warned that the world is almost certain to experience new record temperatures in the next five years. A breaching of the crucial 1.5 degrees Celsius threshold could have dire consequences. Even if temporary, it would send the world into "uncharted territory."

Climate peril cannot be overcome by only reducing CO_2 emissions. Mark Lynas, in *Our Final Warning: Six Degrees of Climate Emergency* (2020), and David Wallace-Wells, in *The Uninhabitable Earth: A Story of The Future* (2019), both starkly point out the disruptive consequences for the planet corresponding to various degrees of warming and the need for any solutions to reflect local and global, societal inequalities in gender, race and income. The United Nations has depicted global heating as an existential threat to humanity due to the increased frequency of extreme weather events, storms, droughts, floods and heatwaves, as well as the destruction of habitats for all creatures both on land and in the sea. Other potential impacts of climate peril include food insecurity, displacement of people and increased risk of disease.

The Conference of Parties on Biodiversity (COP15) in December 2022 identified five drivers of the biodiversity crisis, all of them caused by humans:

1. changes in land use, particularly agriculture.
2. climate change.
3. pollution, including pesticides and plastics.
4. over-exploitation of wild species.
5. introduction of alien invasive species.

A global, intergovernmental assessment of biodiversity and ecosystems concludes that up to one million animal and plant species are now threatened with extinction, many within decades. Some believe that a mass extinction event is underway and that many current life forms could be annihilated, or at least committed to extinction, by the end of this century.

Damian Carrington, in his Guardian article from 24th February 2023, *Ecosystem collapse 'inevitable' unless wildlife losses reversed*,[2] summarises new scientific research that warns, yet again, that the continual destruction of wildlife and losses of biodiversity can suddenly tip over into total ecosystem collapse. Humanity relies on healthy global ecosystems for clean air and water, as well as food. Healthy ecosystems rely on the complex interaction of plants, predators and prey, with each group of similar species playing a unique role. Today, species are being lost faster than in any of the previous five mass extinctions. We may be at the start of a new mass extinction, making total ecosystem collapse inevitable if the losses are not reversed.

Activist group Extinction Rebellion, in their website section *Tell the Truth*,[3] state that, "We are facing... an unprecedented global emergency. Life on Earth is in crisis: scientists agree we have entered a period of abrupt climate breakdown, and we are in the midst of a mass extinction of our own making... Human activity is causing irreparable harm to the life on this world. We have changed the composition of our planet's atmosphere so negatively and significantly that we are jeopardising the very existence of all species, including ourselves."

In 2021, when David Attenborough addressed the United Nations Security Council, he stated that "If we continue our current path, we will face the collapse of everything that gives us our security, food production, access to fresh water, habitable ambient temperature and ocean food chains. The poorest, those with the least security, are certain to suffer. Our duty right now is surely to do all we can to help those in the most immediate danger."

Negative tipping points feature strongly in warnings about the urgency of responding to the crisis.

Many writers such as Lawrence Krauss in *The Physics of Climate Change* (2021), raise the issue of tipping points. These are points or events which trigger a process that cannot in current human timescales be reversed. These include climate warming processes that have gone beyond any possibility of being regulated. Researchers believe that a significant number of tipping points have already been triggered, and more are close to being triggered.

Mitigation and Adaptation

In the face of all of this, what kind of responses are being made?

One is mitigation—the reduction of greenhouse gases. This is what the net-zero targets of many governments are focussed on. Net-zero targets aim to achieve zero emissions and maintain the balance between carbon dioxide emissions and emission absorption. The approach of adaptation includes mitigation methods and ways of adapting in new and radical ways to perils which are already visible, as well as ones to come.

Mitigation operates from the view that the global climate situation has reached the point where we need to face the reality and seriousness of what is involved and from the belief that we can still find solutions.

The Intergovernmental Panel on Climate Change (IPCC) is the United Nations body for assessing the science related to climate change. It brings together thousands of the best scientists from all over the world, working together to synthesise and explain, in accessible reports, the latest global climate research available. It's most recent AR6 synthesis report provides a comprehensive review of global knowledge of the climate up to 2023. It explains how to prevent and reduce the risks of the worst impacts of the climate crisis. The report states clearly that success is feasible only if the world acts *now*. It proposes actions to limit global warming to 1.5 degrees Celsius through rapid and deep emissions reductions across all sectors of the global economy. It provides feasible, effective and low-cost mitigation and adaptation options to scale up across sectors and countries through an "acceleration agenda" involving all the G20: the world's biggest developed and developing countries. It calls on emerging economies to set their net-zero targets as close as possible to 2050 and to phase out coal between 2030 and 2040. Governments are encouraged to reduce emissions and give up fossil fuels, invest in renewable energy and other low-carbon technologies, increase energy efficiency, rethink agricultural methods, restore forests and degraded natural landscapes, develop technologies of direct air capture and to explore other means of repairing the climate.

Undoubtedly, achieving such targets will be very challenging, and many governments are likely to ignore them. Some argue that achieving net zero is too difficult and too expensive. Others hold the opposite view — that the cost of not moving to net zero as soon as possible is unacceptable. The success of mitigation and adaptation attempts depends upon financing the cost, creating new green technologies and whether the pace of introducing solutions can happen quickly enough.

In *The New Climate War: The Fight to Take Back Our Planet* (2021), one of the world's leading climate scientists, Michael Mann, agrees that it is not too late to halt or reverse the rise in global temperatures if appropriate mitigation action is taken on a national and international scale. Mann has faith in current economic and market mechanisms if they are given the necessary incentives to bring about desired changes in corporate behaviour. Incentives include carbon taxes, which he believes will sufficiently hasten the necessary move to net-zero carbon emissions. In a similar vein, Bill Gates, in *How to Avoid a Climate Disaster* (2022), focuses on technological solutions to the problems we face. He suggests market-based solutions to speed up the development and improvement of renewable technologies, some which already exist and others which will need to be developed. His aim is to operate at the level of scale to achieve net zero by 2050. To date, technology has been used to address only low hanging fruit such as generating electricity from renewables. Dealing with emissions from agriculture and aviation will be far more difficult. The time to develop and bring to market key technologies, such as carbon capture and storage, and nuclear fusion, is too short if net zero is to be attained across the world by 2050.

Alan Miller et al., in *Cut Super Climate Pollutants Now!: The Ozone Treaty's Urgent Lessons for Speeding Up Climate Action* (2021), argue that while it is crucially important to continue reducing CO_2 emissions, and to move to a net-zero position, this is not sufficient to avert a nearing climate crisis. This is because CO_2 takes a long time to disappear from the atmosphere once emissions are reduced. CO_2 is only responsible for 60-65% of the warming, with other types of emissions accounting for the rest. Principal amongst these is what Miller calls "Super Climate Pollutants," comprised of methane, black carbon, tropospheric ozone and hydrofluorocarbons (HFC's). While they stay in the atmosphere for less time than CO2, these compounds are more potent and have a faster short-term warming effect. The authors posit that cutting these Super Climate Pollutants is the only way to manage warming in the short term and to avoid crossing some of the climate tipping points.

Deep Adaptation

Deep Adaptation is a term coined by Jem Bendell in his seminal academic paper *Deep Adaptation: A Map for Navigating Climate Tragedy* (2020).[4] This is the perspective that society faces inevitable and imminent collapse and that our way of life has a terminal diagnosis due to climate peril. Bendell claims it is too late to stop the climate crisis and so we need to learn how to live in the face of societal collapse. This involves lessening the harm, saving what we can and creating possibilities for future survival. It will necessitate giving up irretrievable aspects of our current way of life. He defines collapse as "the uneven ending of our normal modes of sustenance, shelter, security, pleasure, identity and meaning alongside the potential, probable or inevitable collapse of industrial consumer societies." He predicts this collapse may happen by 2028.

Jem Bendell offers "a map for navigating climate tragedy" with ways of adapting to the severe disruptions of our lives and societies through recognising their real effect and the degree to which they will make our current way of life impossible and irrelevant. He believes we won't be able to respond to the unprecedented scope of suffering and change with only a few reformist tweaks. He proposes a "post-sustainability" ethic where we give up on the false hope that our society can proceed on its current trajectory and argues that we need to embrace "deep adaptation." He also challenges "collapse denial" and the kind of hope that can be an opiate to keep us from thinking about, and preparing for, what we might have to do if the worst happens.

This is a frightening view to many and may be impossible to take on board for others, as it is predicting collapse within the lifetimes of people alive today. In many circles societal collapse is seen as crazy or taboo. Bendell was mocked, vilified and even demonised by several well-known and respected climate scientists, only supported by a few. Yet his paper was read by millions despite being disparaged as "dread porn" and unscientific. It also inspired the formation, in 2019, of a Deep Adaptation social and online forum across the world.

Deep Adaptation calls for different structures and mechanisms to cope with our unprecedented times — for the strengthening of local communities so they can develop resilience and protect the most vulnerable. He advocates local action for communities to develop their own capacity to survive amidst the collapse and to become self-sufficient. The performance of many Governments suggest that they have neither the will nor ability to protect vulnerable communities in crisis.

If you want to explore his views you might like two online articles Bendell has written, *After Climate Despair, One Tale Of What Can Emerge*[5] and *Hope and Vision in the Face of Collapse: The 4th R of Deep Adaptation*.[6]

I find his five R questions really helpful and have used them to generate invaluable insight with students and people I coach. You may choose to answer these questions for yourself.

1. Resilience: What do we most value that we want to keep and how do we keep it?
2. Relinquishment: What do we need to let go so as not to make matters worse?
3. Restoration: What could we bring back to help us with these difficult times?
4. Reconciliation: With what and whom shall we make peace as we awaken to our mutual mortality?

5. Reverence: What do you want me to know and what do you want me to do?

***

In a similar vein, Rupert Read encourages us to act for mitigation alongside "adopting deep adaptation as the ultimate insurance policy." He advocates riding "two horses" simultaneously in his chapter "Riding Two Horses: The Future of Politics and Activism, as We Face Potential Eco-driven Societal Collapse" (2021). He urges a shift away from the current assumptions of climate activism steeped in a philosophy of sustainability within existing capitalist "false paradigms" as well as going beyond a defeatist, doomerist approach. He believes that civilisation is finished, the catastrophe ahead as inevitable and that we need to act in ways that ensure deep, "transformative adaptation" through clarity and determination rather than give up.

Extinction

Extinction is linked to both the ecological and climate crises. This is the most radical perspective which holds that humanity could become extinct along with most, or all, of the other species. It is widely accepted that we are living through a "sixth mass extinction" event caused by human activity. The UN Environment Programme says there is "no credible pathway" to limit global heating to 1.5 degrees above the pre-industrial level, a figure agreed on at the 2015 Paris Climate Conference.

Elizabeth Kolbert in her iconic book, *The Sixth Extinction: An Unnatural History* (2014), argues that the earth is currently experiencing a mass extinction event orchestrated by humanity. She describes the complete extinction of some species and dramatic reduction in many others. She makes the point that we are in a similar position to that during the previous five extinctions that have reduced or lost species. We are in a sixth extinction because we are now experiencing such an extreme loss of habitat for many species, crushed and destroyed by the human footprint.

Near-term human extinction is a view associated with abrupt climate change and rapid global heating linked to the crossing of climate tipping points. I have explored the more extreme extinction views posited by two climate scientists, Guy McPherson on his website[7] and Sam Carana on *Arctic News*,[8] which both offer extensive information. Their views raise the potential for the extinction of humanity as near as 2026. Near-term human extinction being a possibility is a chilling wake up call even if you disagree with this view.

What About Hope?

As an optimist, I have had to redefine my relationship with hope. I enjoy the paradox of exploring views that clearly evidence that the world is getting worse alongside views that focus on articulating ways in which the world is simultaneously improving. I have enjoyed reading information on how climate peril might be alleviated in time to prevent catastrophe, at the same time I engage with those who believe it is too late, agree with societal collapse, and posit the inevitability of a catastrophic future for humanity. Absorbing this conflicting information into my own stance has helped to alleviate my worries and retain a realistic position without falling into denial.

The human capacity for hope in the face of extreme adversity and potential extinction fascinates me. I understand hope as a feeling of expectation and desire for a particular thing to happen. I have been exploring hope with writers, colleagues and friends who have moved beyond hope and are redefining hope, as well as those who cling firmly onto their hope. I share some of this below.

We all want to survive on a thriving planet, so having to face and accept scientific evidence supporting the potentially destructive and life-ending impact of the climate crisis can disrupt our hope. Some choose to continue to be hopeful in the face of all the dire warnings.

Some mainstream scientists, and even the IPPC, are still arguing that if we rapidly reduce the use of fossil fuels down to net zero then eventually the climate will stop warming. They are holding out hope that the climate peril can be resolved. However, this would not resolve the ecological crisis which would remain. For others breaching the 1.5 degrees Celsius target does not mean that the world cannot be saved or that it will end. It will just mean vastly more suffering and injustice.

Our state of mind affects our perception of what is true and false, exciting or catastrophic. Are you primarily an optimist or pessimist? I am intrigued by climate optimism. Climate optimism is defined as a framework based on the idea that we can restore the earth back to health, and in so doing protect humanity.

Zahra Biabani, a young climate activist, in her book, *Climate Optimism: Climate Wins and Creating Systemic Change around the World* (2023), thinks that people will choose not to believe in climate change if they are overwhelmed and see no way to solve it—the opposite of my own experience. She encourages the empowerment and funding of communities of colour and indigenous communities experiencing the dire consequences of climate change. She explores the generally positive things that are happening in the world and the achievements of climate activists. I really like her book, particularly where she points out the activities of young climate activists in the law courts, successful cases of litigation around clean air, shifts in climate change policies and wins in the market. It is important to be reminded of how numerous individuals and climate groups around the globe are fighting and winning battles, especially within the fields of climate justice and intersectional environmentalism.

She advocates that we all ask ourselves the question, "What if we do?" and gives practical tips for practising climate optimism to inspire young people to act and to be hopeful. She encourages a "sweeping movement to protect the planet and all that inhabit it." She closes her book with the words "as long as we are here on this earth, we must continue sowing seeds of hope, tending to the fertile ground that birthed us, sustains us, and that will be our resting place." She provides insight and practical support through her climate optimism approach to assist young people to continue in very difficult circumstances. It is an understandable and admirable response from a young climate activist on how to keep going.

Antares Gennari, in *The Climate Optimist Handbook: How to Shift the Narrative on Climate Change and to Find the Courage to Choose Change* (2023), focuses on the possibilities we can hold moving forward. She wants to shift the climate change narrative from one of doom into one of action from "courage and excitement, not fear."

Both writers resonate with many people, and I applaud their work. Yet I feel they are missing the importance of our state of being, of presence and of shifting our consciousness into acceptance alongside skilful action. Having said that, I believe if I was still a young person, climate optimism would suit me well.

James Hansen, a well-known climate scientist, in his paper *A Realistic Path to a Bright Future* (2021)[9] encourages young people not to despair in the face of all the difficult and overwhelming news they are bombarded with every day. He praises their acumen and ability to affect national elections and appreciate global issues. He also believes that young people can alter the course of our world in a good way if they understand what is needed. You might feel hopeful reading his paper in full for yourself and reading aloud these words by Hanson.

> Do not feel sorry for yourself or get discouraged. Yours is not the first generation to be dealt a bad hand. Some were born into great depressions. Some were sent to fight in world wars or senseless conflagrations in faraway places such as Viet Nam or Iraq...Your task is now urgent. The next 10 years — the fourth decade since the adoption of the Framework Convention on Climate Change in 1992 — must be the decade in which young people take charge of their own destiny.

Iddo Landau, in an article in *Psychology Today* (2018) titled "5 Ways in Which the World Has Been Dramatically Improving",[10] identifies five major spheres that have improved in recent times.

In a similar vein, Julius Probst[11] provides seven reasons why the world is improving in his online article, "Seven reasons why the world is improving" (2019).

In March 2023 David Attenborough, after making his BBC *Wild Isles* television programme, offered a more optimistic view when he said that he remains hopeful for the future despite the crisis in nature and feelings of powerlessness generated by the scale of the issues facing our planet. He believes that everyone needs to act now—as we do have the solutions—and together we can save our planet.

Joanna Macy, in *Active Hope: How to Face the Mess We're in with Unexpected Resilience and Creative Power* (2022), offers a form of hope as something we do rather than something we have. She has provided a way of coping for millions over many years.

Jen Bendall, in his article *Hope and Vision in the Face of Collapse: The 4th R of Deep Adaptation* (2019),[12] advocates a move beyond the "false hope" of personal or collective salvation towards a "radical hope" inspired by the way in which some Indigenous

Americans responded to accepting the inevitability of the destruction of their way of life through colonialism.

Margaret Wheatley, in *Who Do We Choose to Be? Facing Reality, Claiming Leadership, Restoring Sanity* (2017), encourages people to explore the "place beyond hope," as she believes that hope is "the hottest hot button among us activists" helping us to avoid despair. She advises not cheering or inflating, but just simply accepting where you are, staying there until you find your ground, right there, staring into the darkness. She posits that without the filter of hope and fear, spontaneous right action emerges without hesitation, leaving us able to act with compassion and insight. This is resonant with my Presence Activism approach.

Rupert Read in his Chapter "Riding Two Horses: The future of politics and activism, as we face potential eco-driven societal collapse" (2021), challenges the need for climate activists to be falsely optimistic with a "happy face" to succeed.

Hopium, or hopeium, is a new word blending hope and opium. It means being addicted to irrational or unwanted optimism, with connotations of being annoying and self-pitying. It has been presented comedically as a satirical fictional drug to help people stay hopeful in times when there is none. Its use began in 2010, originating from an opinion piece on stock market investment and extending into online forums featuring Pepe the Frog, bitcoin, politics, climate change and deep adaptation.

Where Do I Stand?

I am naturally a hopeful, joyful, optimistic person, full of energy and enthusiasm, and have been so all my life. I have found facing climate peril extraordinarily difficult. The global situation looks extremely bleak to me. Emissions of CO_2 should be falling but are still rising, and scientific reports predict that temperatures will continue to increase. The World

Meteorological Organisation's (WMO) predicted breaching of the crucial 1.5 degrees Celsius threshold by 2027 should be a massive wake up call. The announcement deeply affected me.

Millions of people have already had to migrate due to changes in their living environment. Problems with agricultural production are getting worse, more people are finding it difficult to access food and water and there is a massive food shortage in parts of the world.

I don't believe in human extinction. I believe that, at the very worst, at some point in the future, the population of the world will be much diminished and there will be pockets of the population living in reasonably habitable areas. No-one will be enjoying the same kind of lifestyle or benefits that we currently have in the most prosperous countries today.

I locate myself within Deep Adaptation, as I do believe that society is likely to collapse sooner than many think, across all fronts, with a breakdown in capitalism as we currently know it. I would like governments, corporates and key influencers to take this perspective on board as a reality and act accordingly at a very fast pace.

I agree with Jem Bendell in his latest book, *Breaking Together: A Freedom-Loving Response to Collapse* (2023), that current thinking within the paradigm of patriarchy and capitalism has got us into the climate mess. The first part of his book describes the nature and process of collapse with all the difficulties involved. Yet, like him, I believe that this collapse also opens the way for a new, radical paradigm and set of responses. Bendell offers a "dual hypothesis". Firstly, that societal collapse is both inevitable and already apparent, creating societal fractures that are deep, widespread and irreversible. Secondly, once we accept the inevitably of collapse, we can better understand the forces which brought us to this point and seek a different way forward, working together and in harmony with the natural world.

Along with Bendell, I too want "a transformation of the whole of human civilisation, everywhere on the planet, and immediately, simply to give the younger generations a slightly better chance of a decent life." I join his call to face seriously this worsening situation and to identify what we wish to save so that we can look critically at the forces which have brought us to this point without recreating the difficulties of the past. The goal is to co-create opportunities for change that will emerge directly because of the drastic break down of current societal norms.

We have to look beyond the absurdity, failure and limitations of technological fixes and face the inevitable impact on society as a whole. In my view, too few of the solutions offered within the existing paradigm of capitalism, especially technological fixes and renewable energy, are likely to resolve climate peril problems within an appropriate timescale.

Some of these "fixes" may even be making things worse, a premise supported by Elizabeth Kolbert in *Under a White Sky: The Nature of the Future* (2022). She visits laboratories and large mitigation experiments all over the world, highlighting the absurdity, ineptness and unforeseen damage from the "Anthropocene irony" of mitigation attempts to solve the climate crisis with technology. She describes numerous specific interventions including the dredging of a canal which "upended the hydrology of roughly two-thirds of the United States," and the introduction of species to solve one particular problem creating unforeseen issues that may be worse than the original problem. She reminds us that Indigenous tribes have been adversely affected, sometimes decimated, by technologies creating ecological crises for centuries. The title of her book stems from the "negative emissions technologies" designed to stave off global warming by deflecting solar heat through spraying reflective particles into the stratosphere. While perceived as a solution, this initiative could damage the ozone layer. This could cause drought, acid rain and bleach all the blue from the sky. She explains her technical analysis of all the dangerous consequences and that all the deferred global warming could return and open a "globe-sized oven door." Some technological interventions are actually making things worse.

My biggest concern is that while there are a range of solutions and opportunities to mitigate and to adapt, however ineffective or inadequate, no government or corporation is acting fast enough or responsibly enough to prevent the potential disasters ahead. I have lost confidence in our patriarchal, capitalist society of greed and self-interest to stop the exploitation and pollution of our planet quickly enough. We need to liberate ourselves from the destructive ideologies enshrined within the current paradigm.

Even if the issue of climate peril is successfully resolved, which seems highly unlikely, there still remains the issue of ecological degradation, which in some ways provides a more difficult problem to solve. I am uncertain on timescales, but the planet will hit many tipping points over the next thirty years. I want sensible and effective mitigation and adaption solutions to continue, as even amidst collapse, they may add value.

I see an urgency to develop local sustainable communities by introducing regenerative farming, securing food and energy supplies in a sustainable way and preparing for a very different future. This is my primary focus. My husband and I have numerous conversations about the best ways of living and what we need to do within our lifetimes to add value for not only our own children, grandchildren, but also for future generations globally, while acting locally. To that end we support our Glastonbury community, and our own village to be more sustainable.

As an activist, I am able to live my life, beyond denial, with acceptance and equanimity while being of service through skilful action, primarily because of the potency and power of presence.

Why Presence?

Presence gives me the capacity to stay grounded, strong and resilient. In presence I can let all the views, facts and figures, warnings, dangers, conflicting positions, fears and anxiety settle, integrate and flow through me, without stressing me. Presence enables me to live as much as possible in the moment and to allow all forms of possibilities to be in my consciousness, with enough non-attachment, so as not be overwhelmed or anxious.

In my experience, activism without inner work may not alleviate anxiety. Presence, which stimulates and encourages our inner work, is the antidote to climate anxiety as it supports and nourishes us into a more sustainable and skilful outer activism.

Until presence became my centre of gravity, I alternated between denial, false optimism, grasping at solutions, believing that governments and corporates are going to act responsibly and quickly enough, and worrying about possible extinction. The worst thing for me was falling into the fear of a horrible dystopian future that my grandchildren, great nephews and nieces may be forced to live in. Even now, sometimes when I am with my grandchildren, I feel a sadness and inability to protect their futures, even shame and guilt that my generation has let the youngsters down so badly. When I gently move into presence, those feelings dissolve and I can return to equilibrium and skilful action on their behalf.

I watch friends and colleagues fall into grief as they journey through their own emotional reactions and understandings on climate peril. I witness people moving into deep denial that stops all conversation other than a false optimism, or into a need for assurance that all will be fine, as "those in charge" will sort it. It seems to me that unless directly and personally affected many people cannot give the climate peril their considered attention.

In this book I share my direct experiences of presence dissolving and relaxing confusion, overwhelming anxiety and fear for the future. In presence, we are held, grounded and we feel safe, whatever the circumstances. Presence expands our capacity to cope with climate peril challenges and to act with skill in the world.

***

Having offered a brief overall context of the climate peril, I hope you will go more deeply into any aspect that most interests or affects you. I discarded fifty thousand words I had written on climate peril for this chapter to focus on the most salient points from my perspective.

In the next chapter I explore understandings and experiences of presence within five domains, illustrating the potency and significance of presence as a means of coping with whatever you are facing and supporting you in taking effective action within an uncertain future.

Chapter 2

Presence

"Awaken to the mystery of being here and enter the quiet immensity of your own presence." **John O'Donohue**

***

Introduction

To understand how and why presence is a potent and profound antidote, in this chapter I ask you to explore your relationship to presence, then explore presence within the five different domains of Personal Presence, Professional Presence, Transpersonal Presence, Nature Presence and Being Here Now. Within each domain I provide an overview of understandings and contributions of presence, then I describe my own experience within each domain. I then describe my own experiences of the transmission of presence.

Presence can change or relax anything, including overwhelming anxiety and fear. It is everywhere, literally everywhere, both inside and outside of us, whether we are conscious of it or not. In presence, we are held and feel safe, whatever the circumstances. Presence increases our capacity to cope with challenges and act with skill in the world.

The Potency of Presence

Through my own experiences of spontaneously being in presence, cultivating presence, receiving presence transmissions and being a presence teacher, I understand viscerally how presence has helped me to be active and skilful within my personal, professional and activist life. It has dissolved my constructed personality, including any anxiety, and has also enabled me to expand my perspectives of reality and my senses of self. As a presence teacher and coach, I have seen directly how my students and coachees are positively affected by presence, and how it has helped them to face climate peril and move through their own anxiety.

My Luminary students, and the people I coach, are inevitably affected by my presence. I consciously implement presence transmission with individuals and in groups. For many years I have been saying that whatever the issue, problem or constraint the answer is presence. What I mean by this is that the more we are in presence, the more we can perceive our interconnection with all beings and with nature. We can act in ways that co-create solutions, especially ones that protect rather than harm our planet. When in presence we have equanimity amidst whatever is happening around us. In presence we gain access to whatever we need to respond skilfully and thrive.

Over the years, many of my Luminary students have told me that they feel more equipped to act, lead and cope by learning to be more present in their lives, especially with the stress of climate peril and living through the pandemic. When asked to comment on my presence teachings, they responded with the following.

***

"Presence. You taught me how to cultivate presence, what it feels like to be seen and heard when you are coming from that place of gnosis, of divine presence. I remember you saying right at the beginning of the Luminary course about the conscious balance of a leader's outer and inner awareness in the room and understanding what percentage of their awareness extends outwards or is directed inwards. This supports the power of your presence. That was exactly the opposite of me, I was always scattered and too buffeted by others' energy! I now understand that in that centred, grounded, deeply coherent state we are fully available to respond to what we hear in a kind of new 'clustered' thinking way, that

allows for multiple new connections between thoughts to arise, offering non polarising solutions of Both/And rather than Either/Or. This has enabled me to offer workshops for women in UEA with a whole new level of depth, presence and impact." **Julie**

***

"Lynne, your gentle lead and your grounded strength. The capacity to imbue at the same time vulnerability and stature, compassion and jolliness, mysticism and concreteness. The way you are present has made me much more present." **Tanya**

***

"I have been a direct-action campaigner for thirty years yet was still seeing my battles through a limited lens. With Lynne's teachings, I explored and dispelled blocks and binds that made me feel unworthy. I learnt how to be more and more in presence, as well as being on the frontline. I now run seminars with activists teaching that they are all leaders in service to the world and how to come from presence and a strong, centred place." **Indra**

***

"Grounded and centred and fully present. One of the treasures I learned from you at the Luminary training." **Marion**

***

"I am continuing to recognise and acknowledge the importance of presence. To stop and breathe and connect to mind, heart, body/gut/ womb. To be in connection to the different parts of myself and to the whole. For me the breath is my bridge. In this way I can come into presence swiftly and with ease." **Cath**

***

I have developed the Presence Flower, a process, described in detail in the next chapter, through which you can consciously work with presence. My focus is on dissolving climate anxiety, as it is such a significant and important issue in the world today. Presence is a profound antidote to anxiety and enables skilful climate activism. The Presence Flower process is not just about feeling better for yourself, it is also about being and acting skilfully, from presence, in the world.

I am a practical person, as well as a mystic, who is nurtured and continually influenced by all my presence experiences. I am also an activist and a leader, wanting to make a difference in the world. I want, and have developed, a balance between being and doing because it feels like the right thing to do. I have always been both a spiritual seeker and a social justice warrior.

In the rest of this chapter, I explore what presence is and what it does, invite your reflection and experience of presence, share my experiences of presence, explore presence through five domains and describe presence transmission.

Your Experience of Presence

I am curious about your experience of presence and what it means for you. I invite you to reflect, here now, on what arises for you when you ponder the word presence. I am most interested in what Presence *is* for you. You may wish to take time to reflect, to journal or to discuss with someone else, before reading any further.

***

I believe that everyone can develop presence if they choose to. For some it arises easily or spontaneously, for others a conscious practice is important.

Presence can only be known experientially, through being present. We can practice presence by collecting our attention, taking stock of where we are and noticing what is happening in this exact moment in our head, heart, body and belly—both inside and outside ourselves. Presence involves direct awareness, in real time, in this present moment. When we are present, we can retain an internal, felt point of contact as we read, listen, act, move and feel. We become more and more aware of the content of our thoughts, sensations, reactivity and feelings. We notice, without staying attached to, or affected by, what is happening in us in this exact moment. It involves all of us being consciously and intentionally here, through a direct awareness in this present moment. There are no rights or wrongs, no particular way to be, simply being present with a witnessing of whatever is arising.

***

I invite you now to be open to a visceral and direct experience of presence. Your own unique direct experience of presence. Don't worry about getting it right; just *be* however you can *be*, here now. All that matters is that your experience is real as you relax, sense, open, allow, observe and deepen. Can you let go of all notions that you should, or need to be, anywhere else, internally or externally? Can you allow the truth of being in exactly the right place and space, here now?

Whatever your previous experience with presence, I invite you to be present, here now, and I offer a process of entering into presence below. If it feels better for you, use your own presence practice.

Presence Practice: Being Here Now

I invite you now to sit, or stand, quietly in silence and to go at your own pace. Notice your posture. Are you comfortable and sitting upright, not too stiffly? Notice your breathing; let it calm and settle into an easy rhythm. Allow yourself to fully relax.

If you can, notice every part of your body. Which parts are tight or stiff? Perhaps tense and relax each part of your body, until your whole body feels in a more relaxed state.

Notice where your attention is. How much is your attention drawn inwards or outwards?

Sense your arms and legs and feet. How much can you sense them directly?

Notice what is happening in your body. As you sense into how your body is being affected, what happens?

Are your mind, heart and body open, or do they feel closed? How are you experiencing each of them? Go fully into your internal experience here now. What is happening?

What is happening in your head? Notice your thoughts. Can you notice them without being drawn into them? What is happening in your heart? Notice your emotions. Can you notice them without being drawn into them? Can you allow all thoughts and emotions?

What is happening in your belly? Overall, what is happening in your body?

Can you allow yourself to notice, to observe all that is arising without being deeply engaged and affected? Can you both experience and observe how you are being here now?

Can you allow yourself to simply be here, in this moment, exactly as you are with no judgement, no editing, no trying to change anything?

***

When you are ready, allow yourself to move out of this practice and let your attention return to the external space you are in, notice the sounds around you. Quietly allow insights and reflections to arise. Journal if you want to. Reflect upon the most important thing for you from this practice.

***

As you continue to read, notice yourself, in this unique moment, reading and experiencing my words. Become aware of what is going on inside yourself, as well as outside yourself.

Notice what is happening. When present we can experience both dynamism and stillness, we can retain an internal felt point of contact as we continue reading.

How I Experience Presence

It has taken me over twenty years to understand how to consciously manifest presence, through experimentation and cultivation, as well as experiencing spontaneous presence. My understanding of the nature of presence has shifted and changed radically over the years. In all the various ways I experience presence, it is always palpable, calming, healing and full of mystery beyond any rational and cognitive understanding.

Currently in my life, I know a steady state of constantly being in presence. I can move consciously, or spontaneously, into presence at any time or place. I have the capacity to access, witness and return to a state of presence, ever more skilfully and speedily. This provides me with an underlying deep sense of inner calm and equanimity.

Presence enables me to cope with the current craziness of the world, especially as an activist. Of course, all the suffering and challenging aspects of climate peril affect me deeply. I feel the pain and distress that surrounds me in my own life, as well as the constant barrage of awful news from all over the world. The horror of accounts of devastation in war, refugees being treated appallingly, extreme weather catastrophes, the ever-growing cost of living, people dying of COVID and other diseases, the daily effects of the energy crisis and the possibility of extinction are a list that constantly bombards me.

I can cope because within all of this drama, I know when in presence, there is a reality of benign goodness and compelling beauty in the natural world despite all the destruction taking place. Yes, I worry for my children, grandchildren and future generations; I want a better world for everyone. I can simultaneously accept, while not condoning and continuing to challenge, what is happening in the world right now as the only place we can be.

***

Here now, in presence I can hear the sound of silence. I can feel presence in the very moment I access or describe it. I can feel it now as I write these words and allow them to be a portal of presence. I feel it in my fingertips tingling with heat and energy. I become spaciousness and expansiveness, my head and heart open wide. I have no boundaries; my body dissolves. I have no need to speak in the sound of silence. I feel calm and know that anything I need will arise. Everything is here now, a deep contentment, all yearning and separation fall away. I connect with presence. I experience myself as presence. Anxiety and worries fall away, I know that all is well and always will be. I feel complete trust, love and strength, able to cope with anything that comes my way. I am open and curious rather than judgmental. My mind, heart and will are spacious, receptive and open. My inner chatter and preoccupations subside into the background.

***

I bring my attention back to writing my book, staying in presence while simultaneously moving into writing about my direct experience of presence. I am both being and doing. My writing flows and I begin to remember other experiences of presence.

In spiritual healing I feel the difference between being an individual experiencing presence, and presence flowing through me as an empty vessel. I feel a flow of hot energy in my hands when I am offering spiritual healing. As an empty vessel, I surrender and dissolve into the energy of presence flowing through me, for my edges dissolve and I feel at one with a powerful healing energy.

I experience presence in ceremony and ritual, in sacred places, in the presence of particular people, with spiritual gurus, in nature, and in love making. As a presence teacher, I co-create fields of presence with others while facilitating courses, retreats, and coaching sessions.

In the deepest experiences of transcendental presence, alone and with others, I have cried, healed, calmed, felt loved, felt stillness, connected with the Divine and experienced myself as the Divine. I have felt awe, wonder, surrender and the peace that passeth all understanding. Presence feels interrelated to my state of being, while also influencing it at the time it occurs. Sometimes I experience presence as a gentle peace that permeates my inward thoughts and emotions, that brings calm to my body. Sometimes I experience presence as joy, as awe and wonder, humility, smallness, healing tears, the passion of being loved, of being love itself. In all the various ways I experience presence it is always palpable, real, mysterious and healing.

Daily I experience a dance, an opening and closing, between being present and spacious and feeling more closed or restricted as my personality habits or constrictions arise and take me away from presence, even though it is always here and immediate.

I experience an ever-growing capacity to witness and access a state of presence, more skilfully, easily and spontaneously. Presence helps me to experience life more profoundly as I stop projecting into the past or future and become deeply aware of my thoughts and emotions.

Defining Presence

In the twenty first century there has been a resurgence of interest in presence. It has become an important feature across many disciplines. It is discussed in many books, podcasts and blogs, both secular and spiritual. Presence is something we can all experience and know, yet it remains fascinating, nebulous and difficult to define.

Faith, wisdom and spiritual traditions over many centuries have explored the role, practice and importance of presence. Modern writers on spirituality are articulating the nature of presence in accessible ways. Presence is also explored within philosophical traditions and the acting, health, creative, teaching, ecological, artificial intelligence, and healing professions. It is expanding as a significant inquiry within modern leadership and organisational development approaches. There is also a growing body of academic research on presence.

The literal linguistic meanings and origin of presence, according to several dictionaries, is from the Latin "praeesse" or "prasentia" meaning to be at hand, being in front of, being for, or being with. The most straightforward definition describes the state or fact of being present, of being literally in attendance, of being physically there in a particular place, alone or with other people. It can also include accompanying someone. In the 16th century, the meaning evolved into carriage and demeanor, still a popular understanding in today's society. The terms presence, being in presence, or being present are often used interchangeably.

Amy Cuddy, in her book *Presence: Bringing Your Boldest Self to Your Biggest Challenges* (2016), explores the responses she received to the question "how do you define presence," which she posed online. She asked if people thought that presence is about the physical, the psychological or the spiritual. Is it about the individual alone or with others? Is it a fixed characteristic or a momentary experience? From the responses received she articulates a spectrum and range of dimensions from the physical and psychological to the numinous and spiritual. She explores how presence can be experienced alone, in relationship, as a centre of gravity or as a mystical experience that takes people beyond their ordinary way of being, and perceiving, in the world.

Despite its nebulous quality, all writers of presence articulate qualities, or competencies pertaining to the actuality of someone's presence. They describe a sense of something palpable and additional which may be described in different ways, yet they all agree that you certainly know presence when you experience it, in ourselves, or in another person. Presence radiates or emanates out from the individual that we recognise as having it. Presence can involve your natural, ordinary, everyday sense of being and existing, and may also involve a boundless, timeless, transcendental or spiritual sense of presence.

Writers on presence who most interest me include: Almaas 2004, Brown 2005, Cuddy 2016, D'Souza 2021, Halpern and Lubar 2004, Hewlett 2014, Ingram 2003, Kirkeby 2000, Rodenburg 2007, Senge 2005, Schuyler 2014, Scouller 2011, Silsbee 2008 and Tolle 1999, 2002, 2003.

I have sought out and met numerous people who have affected me with their presence. These include the Dalai Lama, Mother Meera, Kofi Annan, Pope John Paul II, King Charles III, Thich Nhat Hanh, Hindu Gurus, Buddhist monks, Karen Armstrong, Joan Chittister, Aya Keema, Anita Rodrick, Pope Benedict XVI, Queen Elizabeth II, Prince Phillip, Princess Anne, and my husband. I have been affected by being in the powerful presence of activists, including Nelson Mandela, Satish Kumar, Jem Bendell, Gail Bradbrook and Greta Thunberg.

The presence of each of these people listed above impacted me differently, yet they all had a strong and palpable presence. Some were the most genuine, spiritual, calm and grounded people I have ever met beyond any act or persona, others felt more like a polished personality honed to impact me in a particular way. Can you guess which was which from the list above?

In my ten years, working as an Further Education leader on the national stage, I came into the physical presence of several UK Prime Ministers and cabinet politicians, including Tony Blair, Gordon Brown, David Cameron, Ed Miliband, Nick Clegg, Michael Gove, John Denham and David Blunkett. The only one who had a genuinely inspiring impression of presence on me was Tony Blair, before the Iraq war happened. The rest had a muted effect, with a heavy, sometime toxic energy. One made the hair rise on the back of my neck due to the toxic energy emanating from him.

Five Presence Domains

I have refined my presence inquiry into Five Presence Domains. These are Personal Presence, Professional Presence, Transpersonal Presence, Nature Presence and Being Here Now.

Personal Presence

I use the term Personal Presence to explore the manner and appearance of a person, the presence they inhabit and exhibit within their everyday life. Personal Presence can be described as the qualities and competencies that we have ourselves or are impacted by from another person's presence. It affects the way you carry yourself, how you live, and how you deal with the people around you. Every aspect of your presence has social meaning. When someone has a strong presence, others notice it immediately. We all know the person that turns heads whenever they walk into a room. We may sense that a person of presence has something desirable, often a quality we admire or want, perhaps a hidden quality within ourselves that is seeking expression.

Personal Presence is something that many people are interested in because it can improve their personal life through practical advice on how to dress, act, impress, project and speak.

Presence is often used to describe powerful individuals who energise others with a form of magnetism that is attractive and compelling. They may be the leader you would follow anywhere, and trust wholeheartedly. Celebrities, politicians and popular leaders are often said to have a charismatic presence. Charisma is a term frequently used to describe heroic or admired people. The word was coined by Max Weber from the Greek term "chara," meaning grace, joy and kindness. It's original meaning is defined by Ole Fogh Kirkeby, in *Management Philosophy: A Radical Normative Perspective* (2000), as "a quality that a person may possess that brings her closer to the qualities that characterise the divine."

***

Take a moment to think about someone who you are you attracted to because of their presence. What qualities, behaviours and attributes do they have?

***

Personal Presence is being explored from psychological and physiological perspectives by writers such as Brown (2005), Cuddy (2016), D'Souza (2021), Rodenburg (2007) and Silsbee (2008). These writers have a few differences, yet they all articulate the qualities and competencies of Personal Presence as something palpable which radiates or emanates outwards and can be experienced in the proximity and physical presence of another person. They describe the qualities involved in cultivating Personal Presence: authenticity, gravitas, charisma, communication, connection, equanimity, calm and resonance. They emphasise alignment between physical features like posture and facial expression with verbal messages and presenting oneself with confidence. They also explore authenticity and how the visceral experience of Personal Presence involves understanding and being who we are when aligned to our deepest values, with congruence between words and actions. Having presence involves alignment in our bodily, psychological and emotional facets.

Amy Cuddy, in *Presence: Bringing Your Boldest Self to Your Biggest Challenges* (2016), focuses primarily on the kind of presence that is needed both to persuade others that you know what you are doing and the presence that gives you confidence and engenders respectful treatment. Cuddy suggests that

Personal Presence stems from believing our own stories, and she quotes the words of one of my favourite poets, Walt Whitman, who said that we convince by our presence and to convince others we need to convince ourselves. The stories Cuddy shares are from people with limited resources and low formal power or status, many of whom have experienced intense hardships, yet who still find it within themselves to try to be the best they can possibly be. She explains how being in authentic presence engenders a powerful psychological and physiological state in which speech, facial expressions, posture and movements all align and synchronise. She also defines presence as "the state of being attuned to and able to comfortably express our true thoughts, feelings, values and potential," in a more authentic way of being than any form of manipulation, or of simply managing impressions.

Inner alignment is a key part of the overall process of living our Personal Presence. It involves finding the resonance between all the faculties of ourself, thinking, experiencing, noticing, feeling and subtle sensing. Greater inner alignment always manifests more authentically, with much greater flexibility of action, thought and responsiveness. Cuddy encourages her readers to embrace their own power and to be present in the face of the challenges they face in life.

Patsy Rodenburg, in *Presence: How to Use Positive Energy for Success in Every Situation* (2007), explores presence within three circles of energy. She describes presence as a journey of reconnection which brings forth everything you require to survive physically, intellectually and emotionally. She calls presence "the energy of survival" and gives examples of high performing people who are present, including top athletes.

For me, Personal Presence is about authenticity, and not about adopting, consciously or unconsciously, a false persona to impress others. When someone is trying too hard, or is not authentic, it can make those around them feel uneasy and less trusting. I have worked with many people who try too hard to impress and appear successful, overly full of themselves. They have a very different impact on me than those with authentic presence.

My Personal Presence

I have worked on my Personal Presence for many years, before it became a popular term. People would often comment on how I filled a room when I entered it, and said that I was inspirational and had charisma, so I wanted to find out why they were saying that and what it meant. I began exploring, cultivating and living Personal Presence qualities and behaviours in my own development and in my relationships. I explored charisma, gravitas, confidence, self-esteem, effective communication, self-presentation, body language, power, resonance, emotional intelligence, humility, hubris and integrity. I was particularly interested in body language and the physical alignment and congruence of posture and facial features with verbal messages. I worked hard to present myself fully and with confidence. I always felt that being authentic and congruent were very important. I became inspired by knowing and expressing my fullest potential, authenticity and power. I learnt that the more present and expansive I became, the more I could support and enable others to shine and reach their own optimal potential.

For me Personal Presence has been a useful concept and practice in my everyday life, as well as a pathway to finding the depth of my true self and authenticity. I have developed models of presence and authenticity in my Luminary teachings (Sedgmore 2021). I experience presence in my everyday world when I feel localised presence in my body and through my personality. Personal Presence enables me to function well, to relate effectively and to locate myself more accurately and calmly within the complexity of my life. It supports me on the journey of being the best I can be in my life, activism, work, family, community and relationships. Most importantly it has given me huge resilience, an inner calm and equanimity that helps me to cope with the difficulty of the current climate crisis. I also find that many people trust me and feel I am fair: what you see is what you get. Hopefully that is a sign of my authentic presence.

I have two formal presence practices that I do daily. One is sensing my body through my arms and legs, and the other is focusing my attention, through my belly centre, to directly experience what is happening and arising in the now. I do this twice a day for thirty minutes in the morning and evening. I am also present, as much as I can be, in the midst of action through placing my attention in my body, breath and belly centre, allowing the unfolding and spontaneity of presence to arise, whenever it does, in the midst of whatever action I am involved in.

One of my favourite ways of practising presence is by cleaning my house. There is something profound for me when I focus all my attention on respectfully cleaning the physical objects of my home. My mother raised me to like living in a clean house, to like feeling the satisfaction and sense of purity after a cleaning bout. It has become one of my Personal Presence portals. I have had cleaners over the years, yet as I have aged, I find that cleaning my house is a daily accessible way of being present. I have created more space in my life so that my cleaning doesn't need to be rushed and I can do it at exactly the right time and pace for me. Traveling less during the COVID lockdown enabled me to deepen my cleaning presence practice. It has become such a precious practice to me that I don't ever want to do it in a manner that is resentful or rushed. Gardening is a way of being present for many people: that is my husband's main presencing portal and practice.

Professional Presence

Understanding Personal Presence sets a solid foundation for understanding and being more conscious about Professional Presence. Professional Presence focuses on presence within our workplaces, leadership and communities.

There is a significant literature exploring how to draw on and develop your own Professional Presence in your workplace, particularly as a leader. Professional Presence involves the manner, impact and appearance of a person within a professional setting. It focuses on how to present yourself at presentations or when giving speeches — with confidence and powerful impact. Books on Professional Presence offer guidance on body language, presentation skills, how to dress or speak, how to pay attention to the importance of bodily and facial expressions, and how to pay attention to the way in which you sit, stand and impress others.

Amy Cuddy, in *Presence: Bringing Your Boldest Self to Your Biggest Challenges* (2016), describes how we can self induce presence and makes a very important point about not over managing the impression that we make on others by choreographing ourselves in an unnatural way as a professional. She describes how this is hard work and uses up too much of our cognitive and emotional bandwidth. We may try hard to make a good impression on our colleagues and yet still come across as fake, incompetent, or just not fully present.

Cuddy's approach aligns with the work of Wendy Palmer in *The Intuitive Body: Discovering the Wisdom of Conscious Embodiment and Aikido* (2008). Palmer says that presence is about allowing your body to lead your mind, enabling the most appropriate, timely and right action for any situation or relationship.

Sylvia Hewlett is very explicit about the value of presence for executives in her book *Executive Presence: The Missing Link between Merit and Success* (2014). She focuses on the three dimensions of appearance, communication and gravitas. It is a very practical book based on her research, with case studies of what executives already do, as well as what many want to do to improve their work performance. She includes authenticity as a core characteristic of executive presence.

James Scouller, in *The Three Levels of Leadership: How to Develop Presence, Knowhow and Skill* (2011), sums up leadership presence as the rare but attainable inner alignment of self-identity, purpose and motivation, free from fear. He describes leadership presence which relies upon external factors such as job title, fame, skilful acting or the aura of "specialness" given by followers. Presence reveals itself through a leader as an authentic, magnetic, radiating effect on others. In the workplace leaders gain respect and attention by being congruent, speaking honestly and letting their unique character traits flow.

He recommends a presence not dependent on social status. He contrasts the mental and moral resilience of a person who has "real presence" with the susceptibility to pressure and immoral actions of someone whose charisma rests only on superficial acting and impression skills.

Instead of being seen as healthy, in the workplace charisma can be associated with hubris or a manipulative and disingenuous presence that involves seduction to satisfy one's own professional needs or ends. There are also charismatic people we feel repelled by, or who negatively affect, our nervous systems. I have met many leaders, politicians, members of the UK royal family, famous people and celebrities whose presence has felt hubristic, and had a negative effect on me.

Belle Halpern and Kathy Lubar, in *Leadership Presence: Dramatic Techniques to Reach Out, Motivate, and Inspire* (2004), explore presence as understood within the acting profession. They define presence as "the ability to connect authentically with the thoughts and feelings of others." They claim that not everyone is born with natural presence, yet everyone can develop it. For them presence is "a set of internal and external skills" that flow from within as you learn to discover and reveal your own unique presence. Their process has four acts of being: presence, self-knowledge, expressiveness and reaching out.

Peter Senge et al., in *Presence: Exploring Profound Change in People, Organizations and Society* (2005), and Otto Scharmer, in *Theory U: Leading from the Future as It Emerges* (2009), articulate the notion of presence for executives as "pre-sensing," a mix of sensing and presencing. They have done excellent work to encourage presence in workplaces and have supported a wide range of leaders to connect to the deepest source of themselves in the present moment through allowing their inner leadership and professional knowing to emerge. I have found *Theory U* to be a significant, bridging work between the Personal, Professional and Transpersonal realms.

My Professional Presence

From 1990, I began intense experimentation with being consciously present in my leadership and organisational life. I never wanted to be a lone charismatic leader who was toxic and narcissistic. I had worked with, and had been hurt by, several leaders who led from self-interest and an inflated sense of their own importance.

Michael Joseph completed his Ph.D., *Leaders and Spirituality: A Case Study* (2002), on my spiritual leadership when I was the Principal of Guildford College. He studied my presence, leadership style and actions over a five-year period. He describes how I consciously reflected and worked on my professional presence. He acknowledged how I shared my weaknesses and mistakes through showing vulnerability in public forums, not just in private. He also acknowledged how I gave permission to my colleagues to speak truth to my power, helping me to keep my personality, excesses and flaws in my consciousness and in check.

I have written about leadership and professional presence in my Doctoral thesis, *Fostering Innovative Organisational Cultures and High Performance through Explicit Spiritual Leadership* (Sedgmore 2013).

A beautiful book was given to me as a leaving gift when I left a Chief Executive role in 2007. It includes fifty-seven quotes on how I, as a leader, affected individuals. It includes comments on how staff perceived my presence as described in the three quotes below.

***

"I was thinking about the contribution you have made to our approach to leadership development, Authenticity: the confidence to be yourself, Presence: an ability to stay in the room, Positive energy: a concern to be considered and hopeful. Values driven in everything."

***

"There are some people who are 'unique', they add a presence, light up a room and they make you feel special, valued and in a way 'unique' yourself. I am new to this organisation and in that short time, I have felt that presence."

***

"I shall miss you and your presence, your energy and passion."

***

Over the years I experimented with being more present in work, as well as in my personal life. I had a coach, Simon Western, to support and assist me. Simon's work on eco-leadership as articulated in his book *Leadership: A Critical Text* (2019), has had an immense impact upon me. He describes a leadership paradigm appropriate to a networked and interdependent global environment.

Some of my key transitions in becoming more present are described in Louis Fry and Yochanan Altman's study of my leadership in *Spiritual Leadership in Action: The CEL Story* (2013), and in a description of relationship coaching written by Simon Western and me called *A Privileged Conversation* (Western and Sedgmore 2008).

My constructed personality would kick in at difficult times, yet I was becoming more and more centred and present in my work with colleagues. I was able to access, witness and return to a state of presence more skilfully and more speedily. Moving through my personality defences enabled me to be more fully available, vulnerable and authentic to staff, particularly the ones who most triggered my shadow self. Staff commented that I was calmer, more centred and present in my leadership. I was able to lead beyond my own limited sense of self to a much more encompassing one in which I didn't need to be in control and could trust much more deeply. My personality fixations, behaviours and reactions became less reactive, enabling me to see things, situations and people as they really were in the moment. I began to perceive a clearer sense of objective reality without my internal personality structures and constructs, conscious or otherwise, clouding and influencing the way I responded.

I co-created with others, more liberating, less hierarchical structures and organisational forms, different in intention and shape than ones I had led previously. We brought in facilitators who facilitated presence practices as part of staff development. I genuinely believe this contributed to the extraordinary success of the organisation.

I was privileged to be one of the participants who tell their story of professional and leadership presence, and of no-self, in the book *Not Being: The Art of Self-Transformation* by Steven D'Souza and Khuyen Bui (2021). They articulate powerfully the notion of "not being." Steven has taken the notion and practice of "not being" into a wide range of organisations as a consultant. I have huge admiration for his groundbreaking and exquisite work.

Elmor Van Staden in his doctorate *Leading from Within: The Spirituality and Development of the Contemplative Leader* (2022), included my professional work on presence and spiritual leadership as one of his case studies. He describes how I "developed leadership presence and my sense of self (including no-self) and led innovative organisational cultures through an explicit contemplative leadership steeped in presence. He concludes that to be truly effective, authentic and empowering, a leader needs to bring their whole self into the workplace, being as fully present as possible. He states that presence is an important contemplative leadership quality, often the most difficult quality to cultivate.

Transpersonal Presence

Transpersonal Presence lies beyond the realms of personal, professional and physical presence, while permeating them all. Trans- means beyond or across. This domain is within a realm different from most people's conventional everyday experience. Transpersonal experiences can take us beyond our constructed personality, enabling us to see through our fixed and habitual ways of feeling, acting and thinking. Some people name Transpersonal Presence experiences as mystical, religious, spiritual, unity, peak, enlightenment or oneness experiences.

In this domain presence becomes even more nebulous and harder to define. It can be felt as an entity, an essence, or an energy that is palpably present yet unseen within conventional criteria of physical reality. It involves something being there, beyond the person having the presence experience. It can also be an experience of going beyond one's usual sense of self. This can be felt as a spiritual or religious experience, or as an impersonal universal energy, love, light or a sense of flow.

Transpersonal experience is beyond conventional knowing, indescribable, inexplicable, free of any constructs or naming. It can only be described in hindsight, as the experience itself may feel beyond words.

There are environments, activities and life experiences that can assist our Transpersonal Presence. Some people go beyond their usual experience of self during sporting activities, dancing, lovemaking, walking in nature, singing, writing, playing a musical instrument, praying, being with grandchildren, holding a baby, looking at a piece of art, contemplating a flower, gardening or writing. It may happen in a special place, by the sea, sitting in a temple, walking in nature, sitting on a mountain top, watching a sunset or sunrise—the possibilities are endless.

When presence is experienced as religious or spiritual, there is a sense of something benign, holy, or sacred. It may involve the sense of a personal Divine presence. This can be understood as a male God, a female Goddess, something genderless, or a sense of pure mystery beyond knowing and any kind of construct.

For many, Transpersonal Presence is felt as the deepest, truest and most expansive self, accompanied by spaciousness, boundlessness and expansiveness.

Individuals who experience Transpersonal Presence are affected to a greater or lesser extent, depending upon the significance they give to their experiences. How they respond depends upon their own personality, beliefs or situations. The impact, interpretation and power of Transpersonal Presence can be transformational. In times past, people who were deeply affected were encouraged to leave their daily lives and to retreat on to a mountain top, into a cave, the desert or the forest. Some joined ashrams or became hermits, living in solitude and silence away from other people. Contemporary spirituality and presence may take a different form and can be manifested, as the Sufis would say, "in the marketplace," in our relationships, in our workplaces, alongside our neighbours and in our local communities. This has always been my path, the way of the practical mystic, the person who bridges the spiritual and material worlds, who does not see a separation between the profane and the holy, seeing the sacred in everything. For me Presence Activism is a significant contribution to a healing and transformative activism within the world.

There are many writers on presence from the Transpersonal or spiritual perspective. My favourites include Almaas (2004, 2008, 2014, 2017), Brother Lawrence (1991), Brown (2005), Ingram (2003), Kirkeby (2000), Rodenburg (2007), and Tolle (1999, 2002, 2003).

My Transpersonal Presence

This is what I wrote immediately after a profound Transpersonal Presence experience on the Greek island of Skyros in 1989.

***

Completely suffused with love, total unconditional love for everyone and everyone. Every cell suffused, totally at one, totally unified, within and without. All boundaries between myself and everything around me dissolving. Everything completely connected. Boundless. Beyond skin. Expansive. Deep visceral knowing. Heart knowing, body knowing. Beyond mind knowing. Knowing of true reality as unconditional love, peace and harmony. Profound feeling of wholeness, completeness, of coming home. Fully awake, no preconceptions or expectations. Feeling one with all that is, simultaneously seeing and being the true reality. Benign reality. Goodness everywhere. Everything and everyone is love. Expanding and dissolving into a new reality.

***

Another profound Transpersonal Presence experience happened in 1990 in the presence of Mother Meera, a Hindu Avatar who made a deep impression on me. From that moment onwards, I was fascinated by presence. I describe how her transmission of presence affected me later in this chapter.

Following both experiences, I went to be in the presence of living gurus and well regarded spiritual teachers all over the world. I also read avidly about Transpersonal Presence and learnt to practice presence on a daily basis. The presence teachers and writers who have most influenced me include Bede Griffiths, Aya Kheema, Mother Meera, Acharya Sushil Kumar, Russ Hudson, Miranda, A.H. Almaas and Eckart Tolle.

Transpersonal Presence opened me to a very different kind of knowing, the knowing of my own beingness through immediacy and Presence Gnosis. I experienced presence as everywhere, pervading the universe and constituting it. I experienced having no boundaries, of not being contained within my physical body. My sense of self shifted beyond my constructed personality. I relaxed and dissolved into being boundless, not separate from anything or anyone else.

In 2002 when preparing my ordination vow as an Interfaith Minister, the words "I vow to being presence, in every moment, and thus to serve" spontaneously came to me. I didn't create these words from my mind: I didn't conceptually think them. They arose spontaneously in a heartfelt and soulful manner as a deep truth that I could not fully understand at the time. I chose to go with this visceral knowing and to speak these words as my vow. I am so pleased that exploring, practising and allowing presence to continue arising and flowering has been a central and joyful focus in my life. Each year, for the past fifteen, I have attended two eight-day Ridhwan School retreats which focus on developing and practising Transpersonal Presencing.

Nature Presence

Many people experience presence within nature and on the land. Within the natural world, presence may be experienced as

Nature Presence. This involves an experience of feeling one with and interconnected with the aliveness of natural landscapes, the elements and every aspect of the natural world, with no separation. Nature Presence is an experience of nature being sacred and unifying force and energy. Some experience a flow which has been constantly expanding, creating, nurturing and existing since the beginning of time. Thinking of our planet as Mother Earth or Gaia can make her destruction feel more real and significant.

People affected by Nature Presence often live on islands, or find special outdoor places, where they experience the "air as thin" to foster their Nature Presence. Through the beauty and silence of the natural world, they can access something within or beyond themselves that nourishes and calms. Different forms and expressions of Nature Presence include Neopagan, Pagan, Pantheistic, Panentheistic, Shamanic, Indigenous, Kincentric and Goddess wisdom traditions. These are all are deeply grounded in nature and cultivate presence through, and on, the land, with sacred rituals and ceremonies within the natural elements of air, fire, water, earth, moon and sun. These traditions draw on nature's abundance and the interconnected web of life through the rhythms of birth, death and rebirth. They share an earth-based consciousness of love, respect, honour and nourishment directed towards Gaia, our Mother Earth. They explore and express deep connection, re-animation, enchantment and re-enchantment of our natural world.

I want to honour the Indigenous Kinship or Kincentric worldview, as this is Nature Presence in its purest and most ancient form. Indigenous Kinship is rooted in a deep sense of interconnection and belonging. All beings are recognised as having intelligence and sensibilities. Everyone is a member of interconnected communities and systems that form organic webs and networks of human and nonhuman kin, in which the origin, agency and existence of everything is inextricably linked together. All actions and relationships are viewed as part of an interdependent, reciprocal, universal system or web, encouraging everyone to act as kin to each other.

I am moved by the beautiful book of Indigenous wisdom *We Are the Middle of Forever: Indigenous Voices from Turtle Island on the Changing Earth,* edited by Dahr Jamail and Stan Rushworth (2022). This book is intended to be a support to anyone seeking ideas and responses to climate issues.

The integrated relationship to Earth and its "member beings" is also articulated in *Restoring the Kinship World View: Indigenous Voices Introduce 28 Precepts for Rebalancing Life on Planet Earth,* edited by Wahinkpe Topa (Four Arrows) and Darcia Narváez (2022). It contains important and gracious Kinship worldviews articulating the nature-based consciousness so needed in the world today. It articulates how Kinship can contribute to rebalancing and nourishing all life systems through "harmony between people and other people, and between communities and people and the natural world." The editors state two worldviews to choose from. The Kincentric worldview places all creatures in an interdependent and interconnected part of nature, physically and spiritually. The dualistic worldview separates everyone from nature, physically and spiritually.

I have enjoyed two books by Sharon Blackie: *If Women Rose Rooted: A Life-Changing Journey to Authenticity and Belonging* (2016) and *The Enchanted Life: Unlocking the Magic of the Everyday* (2018). Blackie encourages re-enchantment through seeing the aliveness and beauty of nature and every aspect of the natural world. You may also enjoy Giles Hutchins' book *Leading by Nature: The Process of Becoming a Regenerative Leader* (2022). He advocates drawing upon nature to lead in organisations from the perspective of eco-systems and working collectively in resonance with natural cycles.

I have followed the work of Christian nun, Karen Armstrong, on religion and spirituality for many years and have really enjoyed her new book, *Sacred Nature: How We Can Recover Our Bond with the Natural World* (2022).

One of my favourite writers on Goddess spirituality and of eco-activism is Starhawk. I recommend her work, especially *The Spiral Dance: A Rebirth of the Ancient Religion of the Great Goddess* (1979), and *The Earth Path: Grounding Your Spirit in the Rhythms of Nature* (2006).

Some people turn to a special place or space in nature to find presence and to calm them. This is described in a Guardian article, "When the climate crisis brings despair, I cultivate my inner connection to nature — and find hope" by Claire Ratinon.[13] She describes nature's power to heal and calm her climate anxiety as she works with plants. She writes, "It is through working with plants that I've found an antidote to this particular angst, to pay even more attention to the wonder of the natural world instead of choosing to turn away."

My Nature Presence

I have explored Goddess spirituality for the past fifteen years in the Glastonbury Goddess community, the largest in the world. I have found much of value in this Neo-Pagan tradition steeped in respect for nature within an earth-based sacred relationship with Mother Earth. This has brought me closer to experiencing presence through nature and the land. I feel the pulsating and palpable presence of Mother Earth through my female body. In Nature Presence, I am the embodiment of nature. I feel the creative power of the natural world and the interconnected web and weaving of the whole universe. I am nature and She is me. There is no duality, no separation of any kind. I feel a powerful relationship with the cyclical and natural elements of air, fire, water and earth. I follow the rhythms of nature, her seasons, the moon, colours and smells. I know her fecundity through an interconnected oneness and web of benign nurturing energy that includes beauty, decay, darkness and death. I experience dark and light, depth and height, birth and death, renewal and transformation as complementary, not as opposites or opposing.

I live in Glastonbury, a spiritual vortex and sacred landscape that nourishes me deeply and in which I feel totally at home and present. In the Chalice Well I feel immediately present and open to the beauty, healing and nourishment of the land, the water, the soil, the plants, the insects and a palpable, powerful healing energy.

I also love being in nature where the air is thin, especially on islands surrounded by water. To be restored, I stay in simple cabins close to the sea. Many of my deepest Nature Presence experiences have been on islands: Skyros, Iona, the Scilly Isles, Lindisfarne, Lundy and Bardsey. Stone circles can be deeply powerful, as are the majesty of rocks. Some people will say nature is their cathedral or temple, as it generates the same kind of Transcendental Presence that others feel in sacred, man-made temples and spaces. I remember journeying across Navaho and Hopi lands during an amazing trip in Arizona and New Mexico. The expansiveness and sacred energy were palpable.

I also love forests, especially natural outdoor cathedrals of trees, and had a beautiful experience of forest bathing. The forest was literally singing a symphony in the wind. I could feel the trees in my blood and heart as I existed within a vibrant and exuberant ecological reality in connection with all living things. I now know I was experiencing Biophilia: a term I discovered through reading E. O. Wilson's fascinating book *Biophilia* (1984), which describes our connection with nature. He describes how humans possess an innate and genetic tendency to seek connections with nature and other nonhuman forms of life. I agree wholeheartedly. I know that living in the Somerset countryside, rather than in London, has enhanced my well-being to no end. The changing of the seasons, the sounds, the smells, the fresh air all bring me benefits that city life never did. My relationship with nature is now much deeper and rewarding.

I share below a direct experience of my own nature presence.

***

Walking on the Avalonian Glastonbury land, breathing in the fresh air, gazing into the huge Somerset skies, experiencing viscerally the energy and presence of trees, flowers, plants and hedges. The grass under feet, wind on face, sun on body. The land pulsating with aliveness, whole body tingling. The boundaries between edges dissolving. Body disappearing in the immediacy of now. I am the abundance of white elder flowers along the hedgerow. I am the donkey braying. I am the expansiveness of the open space. I am the astounding green. I am flow, patterns of light shining on the water, the ripples of the river Brue. Dissolved into expansive spaciousness. In total connection, oneness with all of nature. I am Mother Earth, She who births, nourishes and cares for all.

Being Here Now

Being Here Now is being fully in this moment with our whole being and attention. It is a state without the influence of any sense of the past or the future. It is a timelessness within the immediacy of now. A state in which we are free to be present to whatever is happening or arising, internally and externally, in an exact moment.

Being here now includes the realisation that we are always thinking about the past or the future, that our mind has continual conversations with itself that are difficult to turn off. We have lots of opinions, structures, beliefs and concepts, all based on what has happened in the past or may happen into the future. Constant thinking prevents us from enjoying the moment we are in, the moment of simply being here now, experiencing things as they arise new and fresh, freed from all concepts or expectations. This capacity to be here now, whether spontaneous or cultivated, can become a regular and constant state as we learn to relax our personality restrictions, relax our minds and experience presence viscerally and directly.

When we are deeply in presence, time stops or changes from how we usually experience it. We may feel outside of time or within a different time dimension. Our relationship to time changes as we are no longer in chronological, linear, clock time. We experience the unchanging nature of presence and we open to the awareness of no change, and therefore no time.

The direct experience of Being Here Now, fully in this moment with our whole being and attention, can happen though intentional presence practice, it can happen spontaneously or while being deeply engaged in activities we enjoy, with people we love, or in anything that we become fully absorbed into. It may involve the experience of going beyond who we usually take ourselves to be within the busyness of our ordinary and familiar everyday lives.

Ole Fogh Kirkeby (2000), in *Management Philosophy: A Radical Normative Perspective,* describes how the concept of presence and nowness has a "spectrum of philosophical and theological senses" which understand presence as "meeting the eternal in time."

Most spiritual traditions have "being in the now" as a core premise or teaching and recommend living in the moment. Religious literature from early times has explored presence through "being in the now." Brother Lawrence's popular treatise, *The Practice of the Presence of God* (1991), is still read today. I immediately resonated with his daily practices of presence within his monastery kitchen. Presence and nowness also feature in the writings of Christian mystics such as John of the Cross, Theresa of Avila and Hildegard of Bingen. Zen Buddhism is known for its emphasis on "nowness." Hindu, Taoist, Jewish, Muslim and Christian faiths all have transcendental teachings on nowness and presence.

One of the most famous spiritual teachers on presence is Eckhart Tolle. His book the *Power of Now* published in 1999 sold millions; it is a modern spiritual classic. He articulates how we confuse the mind, in its constantly thinking state, with our being instead of seeing the beingness behind our minds. This beingness we may call God, Goddess, source, presence, ground of being, or true self. We are not our thoughts, and equating thinking with our being is to live in separation. By getting in tune with our own beingness, or presence, we can control thoughts and put our emotions into perspective. Until we have control of our minds, they control us. Tolle has supported millions of people to know presence as a very real experience, not just understood as a theory or an idea in the mind. He asks his students and readers to be more present in the minutiae of their everyday life, to see if they can make every moment mean something. Eckart Tolle says that practising the power of now is the path to liberation. In his three books, *The Power of Now* (1999), *Practising the Power of Now: A Guide to Spiritual Enlightenment* (2002), and *Stillness Speaks Whispers of Now* (2003), he describes "now" as a felt oneness in which you are present moment to moment and your attention is fully and intensely in the now. His books are a beautiful synthesis of ideas from Buddhism, Christianity, Taoism and other traditions.

Michael Brown, in *The Presence Process: A Healing Journey into Present Moment Awareness* (2005), provides a fascinating and detailed training of his "Presence Process." He offers practical techniques, perceptual tools and the knowledge needed to heal into and live within present moment awareness. He offers a rigorous and disciplined approach that feels not dissimilar to the twelve steps of Alcoholics Anonymous as he focuses on recovery from addiction within his support and guidance.

Almaas in four of his many books explores how the present moment is not only the juncture between the past and the future, but also the entry into presence, as presence exists only in the moment, beyond the past or the future. He describes presence as a palpable sense of immediacy, of fullness, of hereness through an embodied experience of now in his books: *The Inner Journey Home: Soul's Realization of the Unity of Reality* (2004), *The*

Unfolding Now: Realizing Your True Nature through the Practice of Presence (2008), *Runaway Realization, Living a Life of Ceaseless Discovery* (2014), and *The Alchemy of Freedom: The Philosopher's Stone and the Secrets of Existence* (2017).

How I Experience Being Here Now

I remember the sensation of reading Eckart Tolle's *The Power of Now* in 1992. This was my first deep dive into "nowness." It had a huge impact on me. As I reread my copy, for probably the twentieth time, while writing this book, I noticed the markings and highlights I have made over many years. I am deeply grateful to Eckart Tolle in developing my own understanding and experience of being in the present moment.

The first time I directly experienced timelessness in presence was in 1989 when I realised that time is not linear nor consistent and is related to my subjective experience of time. Sunday afternoons would feel endlessly long for me when I was a child, yet these days, time moves quickly and never drags. Traveling towards a new place on a visit seems to take forever, whereas returning home through the same distance always seems much quicker. Time can fly by very quickly when I am enjoying myself or don't want an experience to end. In presence, time disappears into timelessness and I have no idea of how long the experience has taken when I return back to a more familiar consciousness and sense of linear time.

For me, Being Here Now means going beyond myself into an expansive, non-doing and receptive state. It includes awareness of what is happening in my physical body. I also become aware of my own internal reactivity and personality needs, and how my emotions are being stimulated. I feel fully immersed in what is happening, here now, without personality filters, and I can feel what is most appropriate and skilful in the context I occupy. I access the capacity to be responsive to whatever arises, as well as the ability to see and manifest new possibilities.

The key insight I have gained on presence is summarised by Almaas in *The Unfolding Now: Realizing Your True Nature through the Practice of Presence* (2008):

> Eventually, we recognize that immediacy really means presence. That is, when our experience becomes truly immediate, without the interposition of any mental construct, then we are here, really in the now, fully in our experience. To be in our experience in this way is what we call presence and that is what we mean when we talk about truly being ourselves... and 'being ourselves' turns out to be exactly the same thing, the simplicity of just being here.

Almaas describes my experience far better than I can. I am now able to work within linear time and I can be punctual while knowing, through experiencing timelessness when in presence, that time is not linear.

Presence Transmission

Presence has no form or specific location even though we recognise presence through ourselves or another person embodying and transmitting presence. When a person embodies presence, someone else, just by being in their physical proximity, can receive a direct transmission of presence through them.

Receiving a powerful transmission of presence is hard to describe yet tangible, leaving a lasting impression. We sense a palpable eminence from within and around the person of presence. Something we can sense and feel yet not literally see. It feels transformative, as it is very different from meeting someone's constructed personality devoid of presence. I have had many direct and visceral experiences, with beneficial and transformative effects, of being deeply affected by the powerful presence of someone else.

One of my first and most profound experiences of receiving a presence transmission happened in Frankfurt while meeting with Mother Meera, a Hindu teacher, who transmits through her silent presence without any exchange of words.

***

I stand as they announce Mother Meera is entering. I feel a strong vibration in the air, a pulsation without any noise to it, it gets stronger and stronger. It fills the whole room with waves of energy. She enters, a petite, young and very beautiful Indian woman dressed in a purple sari with long, black plaited hair. A red bindi on her forehead. I feel a wave of energy, a sense of beauty and an overwhelming feeling of flow and dynamism. My eyes fill with tears and my heart bursts open. Expansion in my head. I feel deeply emotional. I am mesmerised, completely enthralled. All of me is affected.

When I kneel before her, and she gazes into my eyes I am looking into the river and flow of the universe. I am filled with love. I feel purified, clean, washed. All my boundaries have disappeared, and I am flowing within a benign, loving, powerful and palpable energy.

***

This was the moment I first experienced a direct and intentional presence transmission. A presence so immensely powerful it changed and transformed my life. Many different things were activated within me. Changes occurred in my perception of reality and my sense of self. I shifted into an altered state of consciousness and the whole experience felt outside of the normal parameters of time, space, and distance. During the four days I visited her daily, I was able to walk across fields in the evening darkness, without any lights. This may sound simple, yet for me it was seismic, something I could never do beforehand, as I feel terror in darkness. On my return home I changed many of my negative actions, behaviours and relationships as I could see the toxicity in them. I can recall the impact of Mother Meera's presence at any time as it remains palpable thirty years later.

Any response to another person's presence is deeply subjective and may differ based on the people involved, their resonance, their vibration and their energy field. The first evening after Mother Meera had left the hall, I asked a woman sitting next to me if she had felt anything and she shook her head. Nothing had happened for her.

This was the beginning of my conscious inquiry into presence, as the impact of Mother Meera's silent presence upon me was extraordinary. I wondered, How was it possible that someone could affect me so deeply? How had she helped me to experience presence so clearly? How was it transmitted? I continued my inquiry by receiving presence transmission from other spiritual teachers from all over the world.

When I met Pope John Paul II in the Vatican synod as part of an international interfaith conference, I must admit to feeling skeptical in advance. I wasn't expecting a profound presence. I had decided he was an out of touch patriarch rather than a holy person. Yet, when he held my hands in his I was filled with an overwhelming and beautiful feeling of love and the most amazing kindness. I can still feel it now as I write these words. I felt love and kindness emanating from him, through his hands, into me. I also felt a deep relaxation in every cell of my body and the sensation of softening. He did speak to me, yet I have no recollection of his words as the sensation I was experiencing was so powerful. After he moved away I felt love for him, and for everyone in the room. I can remember thinking, and feeling, that he was truly holy, even when I hadn't really wanted to.

The presence of the Dalai Lama felt different. He emanated lightness and joy, with a smiling face and penetrating eyes. I could feel myself smiling as he held my hands in a friendly warm embrace. I felt an uplifting and infectious joy.

In 2000, I was a participant in the United Nations Millennium World Peace Summit for Religious and Spiritual Leaders. It was the most extraordinary event I have ever attended. I was in the presence of one thousand men and women, most of whom had a powerful presence. The highlight for me was Amma, the hugging mother, who exuded love and had an energy field of love all around her. As I listened to a speech by Kofi Annan I began to cry. His words were beautiful, yet I was affected mostly by the sense of peace and trust that washed over me and filled my whole body because I was in his physical presence. I felt safe, with an inner glowing of warmth in which I could rest on a deep, soulful level.

Even from a distance, the strength, resilience and wisdom emanating from Nelson Mandela when he gave a speech in Trafalgar Square was palpable.

Thich Nhat Hanh, a Buddhist monk, gave a Dharma talk in London where he exuded peace and calm. I loved how he rang a bell every few minutes while speaking to bring us all into presence with him. I recall a level of peace in his presence unlike any I had experienced previously.

I undertook a two-year training as an interfaith minister because the beautiful and powerful presence of Miranda felt compelling to me. All the presence transmissions described above happened through being in close physical proximity, physical touch or looking into eyes. Each of the presence teachers seemed confident, calm and comfortable in their own skin, with an ease about them. I felt their gestures and presence, while individually different, were congruent with their teachings. I felt seen and was given their full attention in the moment of exchange. They all exuded love and openness; they felt authentic and affirming to me. What I experienced with each of these people was something palpable, an energy field, a sense of the sacred, a radiance, an emanation. They were a portal into presence for me.

Transmission can also happen from a distance through a photograph, a dream, a recording or a book. The presence of Bede Griffiths, a Christian monk, affected me even before

I met him in person. A flyer came through my door with his photograph on it. I had never heard of him, yet as I looked at his image I felt affected. His presence emanated out of the photograph. I knew that one day I would be in his presence. He lived in India, to which I could not afford to go at that time. I bought all his books and followed his teachings for many years. When he came to London I sat in his presence and couldn't stop crying. I felt safe and held. I remember sitting in front of him while he talked, no longer listening to his words, just being completely suffused with feeling safe, tears rolling down my cheeks in a gentle, healing cry.

I first saw Aacharya Sushil Kumar, a Jain monk, in a dream before meeting one of his disciples, Bawa Jain. I was deeply affected by seeing his photograph, hearing recordings of him chanting, holding a mala (prayer beads) he had worn, visiting his temple in India and attending his ashram in the US. Although I never met him in the flesh, his presence deeply affected me and drew me into the ecological nonviolent teachings of the Jain faith.

A mala given to me by the Buddhist nun, Aya Kheema, many years ago still enables me to feel her presence when I hold them for chanting.

I have also gone to teachers whose presence had no effect on me or I felt a dissonance in their presence while other people were having deep and powerful positive experiences. From these experiences I understood the importance of resonance and vibrational energies being aligned or not.

Every transmission was different in kind, and I continued over twenty years to be in the presence of wise people so I could keep expanding and liberating my own presence. Their presence made it easier for me to experience presence, not only with them, but also when alone. My personality, with all its baggage, shadow and inner noise was dissolving through the receiving of presence. I felt like a sponge constantly absorbing presence and emptying out negativity and anxiety.

I no longer depend on the presence of others as I can access presence directly myself. Having said that, being in the presence of my current teacher, Almaas is always beautiful and expansive. He has a purity, incisiveness and expansiveness that consistently melts and illuminates me. I continue to learn from his physical and online presence, as well as from his books.

Each of the transmissions above deeply affected me and I was transformed by being physically close and receiving the energy, essence, radiance and impact of their Presence.

Appendix I *Chronological Stages, Presence Gnosis, Impact of Presence and Transformation of My Personality*, includes a table that outlines the chronological stages and impacts of my presence experiences and journey. It describes the timescales, the nature of my Presence Gnosis and the impact of presence on me, including the transformation of my constructed personality over many years. I include this chart to assist in your understanding of how presence can benefit and transform your life in different stages.

***

I hope you have enjoyed my approach to understanding and experiencing presence through the five domains. Perhaps you feel encouraged to explore, or articulate more facets of presence within your own life and activism, especially presence transmission. In the next chapter I share my Presence Flower as a process for anyone to understand, cultivate and benefit from presence generally, and also as an antidote to anxiety in the face of climate peril.

Chapter 3

The Presence Flower

***

"Instead of bracing yourself for the perils of the unknown, embrace the joy that is here, in your present moment."
Michelle D. Rosado

***

Introduction

My explorations with presence have stimulated me to develop the Presence Flower, created from my own process of the unfolding of presence and its impact on how I live my life as an activist. The Presence Flower process has served me well over many years in living an intensely active life which is also centered and present. I hope that it will support and guide you in your own life, and activism, in these complex, turbulent and stressful times we are living in.

The Presence Flower process is designed as a flower, which you can enter at any point to access its wisdom. It is designed as a nonlinear, circular, spiraling and female process, accessible from wherever your unique journey with presence is. It is developmental and can be drawn upon both as a formal practice and amidst the real time of activism.

I was inspired and influenced by Otto Scharmer's *Theory U: Leading from the Future as It Emerges* (2009), which I studied for my Doctorate. In two of my organisations, I experimented extensively with the U curve as a Chief Executive. Theory U has been hugely popular globally, and the work of the Presencing Institute is impressive.[14]

My Presence Flower is also influenced by the teachings of A. H. Almaas and his Diamond Heart or Ridwhan school in which I have been a student for fifteen years. Almaas combines modern psychological understandings and ancient spiritual wisdom, articulating his current, direct presence experiences, as well as those of his students. His teachings on presence are delightful, deeply profound and have strongly influenced my own journey of presence. I especially enjoyed how he articulates the unfolding of essence in his book *Essence with the Elixir of Enlightenment: The Diamond Approach to Inner Realisation* (1986a).

The Presence Flower provides a clear process to encourage and foster your own unique unfolding of presence. The flower may look complex at first, yet as I guide you through it, I hope the interconnecting dimensions will become clear. It may help to view the flower as a hologram, which you can enter and explore from any layer or petal. There are five layers, and any layer can be accessed and experienced in any order. Begin with whichever of the layers most resonates with you and piece them together to suit your presence practice. The possibilities, sequences and permutations are numerous. Allow your own process, understanding, practice and flow to manifest.

This chapter describes in detail layer 1, Presence Gnosis; layer 5, the Presence Portals and layer 3, the Presence Essences. Layers 2 and 4 are described in Chapter 6 and Chapter 7, respectively. They follow from information on climate anxiety, the Anxiety Flower and activism in the next three chapters. I have structured the chapters in this order to facilitate the integration of presence within the living reality of activism in the world.

Presence Flower Overview

The Presence Flower is illustrated in figure 1 below. The presence process unfolds like the petals of a flower, growing, arising, unfolding and perfuming, as does a natural flower from its centre.

***

There are five layers moving outwards from the centre.

1. Presence Gnosis: how we viscerally know presence.
2. Two Presence Impacts: how we embody presence in the world and how it illuminates our internal perceptions.
3. Seven Presence Essences that arise and unfold to support us in our lives.
4. Six Presence Results: three ways we can embody activism, and three ways we perceive ourselves and reality.
5. Six Presence Portals: ways in which we can access presence.

Figure 1 Presence Flower

Presence Gnosis (layer 1)

At the centre of the Presence Flower is a direct, visceral experience of presence, something I name Presence Gnosis. The meaning of gnosis is a direct and visceral knowing derived from direct experience. It is a deep, profound, subjective, personal truth that feels palpably real. Presence is more visceral than belief, you know it when you know it, in every cell. A noetic knowing that never leaves you. I can recall experiences of presence many years later with a profound immediacy that still has a visceral impact, as the experience remains alive in my whole being.

Presence Portals (layer 5)

I explore the portals second as they are an outer layer and a key to how we access presence. The six Presence Portal petals enable us to skilfully and consciously journey and transition into presence. They invite a slowing down and quietening to foster a deepening beyond all conscious thought, emotions and distractions. You might want to remember them as ROSDOA.

Relaxing
Opening
Sensing
Deepening
Observing
Allowing

Presence Essences (layer 3)

The seven Presence Essences are powerful, potent perfumes or qualities of our deepest nature that arise when we are in presence. They enable us to live our lives free from anxiety and stress. How do we access these? Through the Portals and through Presence Gnosis.

Joy

Peace

Trust

Strength

Resilience

Love

Flow

Presence Impacts (layer 2)

The two Presence Impacts of Embodiment and Illumination occur when we are regularly practising or spontaneously experiencing presence. They support us in integrating and bridging skillfully between our inner and outer worlds. Embodiment supports us to act and live skillfully in the world through presence. Illumination enables us to expand our views of reality and our senses of self. These are described in more detail in Chapter 6 and Chapter 7.

Embodiment

Illumination

Presence Results (layer 4)

When we are impacted by presence on a regular or constant basis, we discover the six Results which stem out of the Impacts of Embodiment and Illumination. The first three influence our actions, and the second three dictate our inner perceptions.

Service

Right Action

Healthy Relationships

***

Interconnection
Views of Reality
Senses of Self

***

Presence Gnosis

At the centre of the Presence Flower is Presence Gnosis—a
direct, visceral experience of presence. Gnosis means a direct,
visceral and noetic knowing which gives us the capacity to
live from presence. It influences and permeates the state of our
whole beingness. It is a deep, profound, subjective, personal
truth that feels palpably real. It may not fit into any concept we
know with our rational mind. It can be difficult to articulate,
yet we know it without any doubt. Presence Gnosis is our
personal truth, experience and knowing of presence as a living,
breathing, palpable experience. Each person's Presence Gnosis
is unique. It can involve experiencing presence within any of
the five domains articulated in Chapter 2, (Personal Presence,
Nature Presence, Transpersonal Presence or a sense of Being
Here Now). I described my own Presence Gnosis throughout
Chapter 2. There is no right or wrong experience of Presence
Gnosis, no better or worse. It's purely our own unique, direct,
visceral knowing of presence in the moment.

Presence Gnosis can be what many people over centuries
have named a peak, mystical, spiritual, religious, nature,
transcendental, self-actualising or enlightenment experience.
Presence feels subjectively real however it is experienced. It
has a palpable quality with a powerful "thereness" or "isness."
William James in *The Varieties of Religious Experience: A Study in
Human Nature* (1994), describes how deeply convincing religious,
or presence, experiences are to the person who has them. They
override logic, feel deeply true and "you cannot help regarding
them as genuine perceptions of truth, as revelations of a kind of

reality which no adverse argument, however unanswerable by you in words, can expel."

The most important thing is to cherish and own our own unique experience of Presence Gnosis. For some of us it takes a while to absorb, acknowledge, understand and integrate such experiences. While many people have them, it isn't always something openly talked about in everyday conversation. We may be surrounded by people who have no notion of what we are sharing.

All sorts of emotions may assail us in the first stages of our Presence Gnosis as it dissolves our constructed personality, especially anxiety and negativity. Presence Gnosis opens and relaxes us sufficiently to impact and dissolve what needs to be let go, to allow us to heal, and to expand in presence.

A significant part of my coaching work is supporting individuals who have had some kind of transformative presence experience that they don't know how to handle. Some of them are in significant positions of power in business or public life. They find my sharing of my thirty years' experience of living presence in organisational life to be useful. I have become a teacher and coach of activists and leaders who are cultivating presence while working in organisations or local communities. I always encourage people in the early stages of Presence Gnosis to find a network of other people who know what it means to travel this journey and have had presence experiences themselves. I was fortunate to have a wide range of people who stepped forward to help, support, advise and guide me along my presence journey. I pay this forward by supporting others.

The Six Presence Portals

The six Presence Portals form the outer petals (layer 5) and are ways in which we can access presence and the essences when they are not arising spontaneously. The portals support us to relax, open, sense, deepen, observe and allow (ROSDOA) into presence. They invite a conscious slowing down, quietening and sensitivity. They enable us to journey and transition into presence, moving us beyond our mind, heart and body sensations and preoccupations into presence. These portals enable anyone to relax into the deepest level of presence of which they are capable in any particular moment. Presence unfolds through each of the six portals like the unfurling of a flower. There is no set order, as they all assist presence as needed. Draw on whichever feels most valuable in any moment. When one, several or all six portals open, presence can be viscerally experienced.

With practice, accessing the six portals becomes easier and more habitual until eventually we find ourselves being constantly in presence. It helps to practice one or more of the six portals as a daily formal presence practice, integrating them into everyday life. Everything can be an opportunity to practice presence. Initially, most of us find it easier to access the portals if we are in a quiet, conducive space in privacy and safety.

These processes are in the outer petals because they may or may not be necessary to experience presence, as sometimes presence happens spontaneously. Creativity and absorption in any activity can enable an organic, unconscious deepening that takes you into presence.

Relaxing

There are three primary ways to really relax: through the breath, our body and our nervous system. The key is to be conscious of our breath and to inhale and exhale slowly and deeply. Then one must allow the breath to fall into a natural rhythm. Counting breaths in a concentration practice helps many people. Relaxing our bodies can be done by tensing then relaxing every single part of the physical body, one by one, starting with our head and moving down to our feet, focusing on parts of the body that are particularly tense.

As explained in Appendix II, *The Physiology of Calming Our Nervous System and Brain,* learning to move consciously into our parasympathetic nervous system can be useful as part of deep relaxation.

It helps considerably if we can be as relaxed as possible in our mind, heart and body, or at least in one of them. The more relaxed we can be the more likely it is that we will stay focused, avoid distractions and be able to access one or more of the essences in presence. When we relax, we acquire the capacity to be still and if necessary to wait, then wait some more, until all the veils and barriers that keep us disconnected from presence fall away. Once this happens, we experience the subtle realms and discover our own Presence Gnosis.

Opening

We may spontaneously open to presence without conscious effort; this can happen anytime, anywhere. Conscious opening is an internal focus of fostering a sense of spaciousness, a literal opening in our heads, hearts and bellies. When I bring my attention to the inside of my head and feel it open more and more, I have a sense of endless expansion, sometimes with a shimmering or the sense of having no top on my head, or even of my head disappear, leaving endless spaciousness. Bringing opening to my heart, I feel my heart expand. It can feel huge, reaching outwards to encompass everything and everyone. Similarly, my belly becomes expansive, with a huge open capacity and a sense of being firmly stable, grounded and spacious. This spaciousness enables me to remain open to whatever arises in, through and around me.

Opening gives more room for whatever we are thinking, feeling or sensing. When wide open, we can let ourselves have any experience. We remain open to any form of fear, pain, suffering, bliss, anxiety, joy — whatever arises. It may be powerful or mild and ordinary. Keeping our attention on spaciousness opens us to presence until openness becomes more powerful than any sensations or preoccupations. Being fully open to every experience can become a dynamic, flowing, stretching, nourishing experience, as being present in the moment reveals itself without any preconceptions.

Sensing

Sensing is more of an embodiment process and is done by putting our attention and focus into every part of our body. It is different than relaxing, as we sense into our body rather than tensing and relaxing.

Sometimes I can sense my body immediately, noticing a particular sensation that needs attention. If I need to cultivate presence, my most effective portal is sensing. For me sensing is literally placing my full attention inside the body part I am sensing.

I share below the sensing practice I have been doing for fifteen years within the Ridwhan school. Do it as slowly and consciously as you can. If your sensing strays into thought, just return back into the body part you last sensed.

Sense into your left foot by sensing into it: literally experience the bottom of your foot, sense it directly, then sense into your toes, one at a time, then sense into your whole foot, then your ankle, then up your calf, into your knee, thigh, buttocks and hip. Continue with full concentration and sensing into each body part, moving from your hip into your left hand, sensing each finger, then into your wrist, elbow and shoulder. Move across to your right shoulder then down through your right side of each body part, mirroring what you did on your left side—sensing down into your right elbow, wrist, hand and fingers. Then into your right hip, down through your buttocks, thigh, knee and into your foot and toes. After sensing the bottom of your right foot, sense into both feet simultaneously, then into all of your body. Notice your breathing and nervous system and allow whatever is arising to be within a deeply sensed present.

Deepening

Deepening is the ability to literally go deeper and deeper into presence, beyond all images, sensations, preoccupations, blockages and restrictions. It enhances, expands and accentuates in a downward movement internally. I have included this as a portal, as many people go up and out of their bodies in Transpersonal experiences. For me presence is a profound depth experience as much as a boundless or upward experience. I find it powerful to be deep in my body and in presence, beyond mind and emotion. Focusing on your breath may help if you struggle to deepen. Sensing into my belly allows me to literally drop into presence. In diving deep we can feel the more subtle layers of inner experience while gradually moving through them.

Observing

An important element of becoming present starts with observing what is happening inside ourselves. This involves observing exactly what is arising, and what we are noticing. Some traditions call this witnessing. It involves suspending any kind of judgement and finding some distance from what is manifesting on the surface. It is not bypassing or cutting off. It took me a long time to understand the difference between detachment and non-attachment. It is non-attachment I am referring to here, simply observing and noticing what is here now, without any projection or reactivity. In our busy, daily life, we can be out of touch with all that is happening. Our attention is usually absorbed with thinking, ideas, concepts, prejudices, memories, beliefs, hopes and knowledge received from our perceptions and inferences. Our default attention is our busy, monkey minds, oblivious to the more subtle sensations that are also arising or the capacity to go beyond them all. Our attention is rarely with what we are experiencing right here and now. Observing assists us in noticing without taking a viewpoint or prioritising one thought, feeling or sensation over another. It simply lets any inner activity arise and fall away. Some people observe their thoughts or mind commentary as if they are passing on a screen. They begin to question who is doing the observing. Just observe until you move into presence.

Allowing

The inner movement of allowing involves embracing what is right here, before us or inside us. Allowing is a movement that follows when our minds, hearts and bodies are open and judgement has been suspended. We become more flexible in what we can perceive, including the subtler layers of our experience. It can be an embracing of what has previously been filtered out as meaningless, unimportant or overwhelming.

The word allowing may be seen as the opposite of rejection, a pushing away of something or someone. Allowing goes beyond any polarity. In my experience it involves not grasping or holding on to anything, remaining fully content with being here now and not seeing or wanting any opposites—no good or bad, right or wrong. We can be with whatever is here, being totally accepting and content with it. We accept any and all experiences or sensations without any need to judge it one way or another. Allowing makes room for everything that is arising; we stop wanting to get somewhere and we cease to need specific, desirable experiences. We truly understand that there is nowhere to get to, so there is no point in striving to get to where we already are. We allow where we are to be unique and perfect.

The Seven Presence Essences

Practicing Presence Gnosis and the Presence Portals opens us to an arising of the seven Presence Essences. The source of all the essences is presence. They can arise in and through us as different qualities and flavors. The more you practice presence, the more these essences will arise as needed for your inner and outer life.

Essence means the essential, basic, ultimate and unchanging nature, element or quality of someone or something. I am using essences to describe the essential states of our souls, the very core of beingness, written about in many different faith, esoteric and spiritual traditions. Our essences can only be known when experienced directly. We cannot use our will to make the essences arise; they are not an object to go looking for. We can only be present, open, spacious enough for them to arise.

They are aspects of our deep nature usually hidden or made inaccessible by our constructed personality. From childhood we obscure and lose experience of the essences as we gradually construct our personality with mental concepts, structures, beliefs, emotions and patterns. Our personality forms to protect us, to cover our vulnerability, our sense of deficiency and to enable us to function in the conventional, everyday world. Our constructed personality has an important survival role. The essences support our nervous system to relax, moving us into a virtuous cycle. The more we can relax our personality, the more essences will manifest as needed, spontaneously or through cultivation. They dissolve structures and our blocked anxiety energies through a pure loosening and disappearing beyond rational understanding.

When we experience one or more of the essences directly, we know that we are presence, the universal flow, the source of life itself. The essences can be experienced as an arising of energy with a distinct impact, affecting your body, heart, mind, spirit and soul.

Initially we may not able to maintain experiences of essence as an everyday reality or centre of gravity. What happens as we get more glimpses and experiences of the essences is that we find ourselves naturally accessing them, and eventually we can abide in them as they become constantly available to us. The essences are powerful and potent perfumes of the soul.

We may prefer certain essences and may find some easier to access than others. In presence, one, several, or all the essences can arise to provide support in whatever is happening or needed in any given moment. They arise through us, are us and are also more than us. They will illuminate our life, behaviours, responses and state of being. Their exquisite impact means we can live more and more in alignment with them. The essences are pre-conceptual and pre-verbal and as we learn how to access them more frequently, we are able to abide within them, coping with and responding to whatever comes our way.

I have synthesised my experiences of Presence Essences into joy, peace, trust, strength, resilience, love and flow, all included in the Presence Flower. I chose these seven because I believe they are the most significant qualities needed in the world today to live and act skilfully, effectively and with equanimity as an activist.

Flower essences are infusions made from the flowering part of a plant. The process of sun steeping or boiling the flower in water captures the energy imprint of the flower and its healing vibration. Every flower has a different healing quality and is a catalyst for change. One of my favourite places to experience presence and a deep healing energy is the Chalice Well in Glastonbury. I have spent much time there reflecting on and writing this book, being as present as possible. The nine Chalice Well vibrational flower and tree Essences[15] are very potent and powerful. I decided to map them onto my own Presence Essences. I hadn't consciously made a direct connection until I had nearly finished writing my book. When I did, I was pleasantly surprised how similar they were. The Chalice Well Essences are offered as "an ally supporting us to become who we want to be, to fulfil our purpose and create the life we want to live." I list them below and also include their healing properties at the end of each of my individual Presence Essence descriptions. The Chalice Well Essences are Pan (joy), Pacem (peace), Beech (trust), Oak (strength and resilience), Blend of Roses (love), Essene (flow), Solomon's Seal (embodiment), Star of Bethlehem and Purple Allumi (illumination).

I now explore the potency, experience and value of each Presence Essence to assist us in thriving in our chaotic and challenging world, reducing climate anxiety and being able to face climate peril.

Joy

The joy essence opens us to delight, curiosity, openness, exploration, gratitude and vibrancy. Unadulterated joy gives us a genuine "joy de vivre" just for being alive. Have you ever experienced moments when for no reason at all you fill with an overwhelming joy and gratitude just because of the simplest things in life? Can you feel gratitude and joy in family and friends, animals, nature, the little pretty delicate flowers that push their way through the pavement, the feeling of wind on your skin, the taste of delicious food or the refreshment of water? Any of the thousands of tiny things that make up your world can be your own unique joyful pleasures.

Young children are easily in touch with simple ways of finding joy. They play wholeheartedly for hours with pebbles on a beach, with the cardboard box of a present rather than the present itself, laughing, giggling and being curious about everything. This is the joy essence, alive and flowing, stimulating a deep and innocent curiosity, playfulness and gratitude. In the joy essence, as adults, we delight in discovering the truth of our authentic potential, beingness and expression. We remain curious even amid difficult times, seeking the learning and wisdom from adversity.

Joy essence is the creative dynamism of the universe, engaging us in the fullness of life. We become playful, inquisitive and light, in touch with natural flow and continual change. We feel our cells constantly renewing, experience the world, and find ourselves as completely fresh and new, every moment in a continual, creative dynamism. The more we are in touch with joy essence, the more we can be in flow. The joyfulness of this essence has an intense sweetness, vibrancy and aliveness, with a delicious, stimulating, tingling energy.

I have always had easy access to awe and wonder, I feel it was always present for me since I was child, and I have never lost it. Even today I find it easy to listen to music or look at a beautiful scenery, sunset, full moon or painting. Each of these can open my awe and wonder. This is sometimes accompanied by a deep surrender, a bowing to something wondrous that is both me and more than me. It is this joy that enables me to see through and beyond the awful suffering in the world, the crazy, irrational wars, crime, harm and sadness. My joy essence never goes away, and I can always access it. It energises me to move beyond any anxiety, exhaustion and difficulty. Activists who can access the joy essence can delight in the everyday and ordinary, rather than in false hope or denial. They can still experience joy in the face of potential extinction amidst climate and environmental emergencies.

A book I love is *Awe: The New Science of Everyday Wonder and How It Can Transform Your Life* by Dacher Keltner (2023). After twenty years of seeking the answer to the good life, and to happiness, he claims to have found it in the capacity to feel and express awe. He defines awe as "the feeling of being in the presence of something vast that transcends your current understanding of the world." He views awe as an ennobling experience that can foster wonder, creativity and collaboration. His book explores awe across many arenas of life and different cultures. He talks to mystics, artists and prisoners.

Dolly Sen is an artist and mental health activist who lives in the UK. Her activism includes laughter and humour, through art, as a way to protest and to inform. Her art is colourful, subversive, satirical and edgy. The Dalai Lama as both a spiritual leader and an activist for Tibet radiates joy with his humour, his smiling face and his eyes.

The aligned Chalice Well Essence is Pan, which "helps us to discover a lightness of being, and to find an irrepressible joy for life."

Peace

Peace essence gives us the deep visceral knowing that "all is well and always will be well."

It calms and dissolves anxiety and stops the busyness of our monkey minds. Feeling calm and peaceful relaxes our nervous system as we genuinely feel in our bones that everything is and will be completely fine. Some call this experience of essence, the "peace that passes all understanding." It is the essence from which the sharing of peace blessings such as "peace be with you" and "Om Shanti" originate from.

When we can access the peace essence, we find equanimity even amidst suffering, fear and loss: a tranquillity so deep that we are anxious about nothing. While this essence feels beautiful, it also assists us to be more efficient and effective in whatever we are doing.

Peace can also be experienced as "the still point" as articulated by the poet T. S. Eliot in his famous poem "1. Burnt Norton" from *Four Quartets*.[16] He describes an experience of being perfectly still at your centre regardless of what is happening outside you. My six favourite lines threaded throughout the poem are: "What might have been and what has been / Point to one end, which is always present." and "The stillness, as a Chinese jar still / Moves perpetually in its stillness." and the most well-known lines, "Except for the point, the still point, / There would be no dance, and there is only the dance." Every time I read this beautiful poem I find something new.

I remember experiencing the "still point" while looking at a huge flower painting by Georgia O'Keefe in the London Tate art gallery. I was mesmerised, and the encounter felt sublime. I was taken spontaneously to a place of profound stillness and felt completely present. My sense of any past and future collapsed into an eternal, present state of peace and stillness within my gaze on her exquisite flower. The moment felt full of grace and beauty, and I can recall the experience immediately, and it still impacts me.

Inner peace, regardless of what is happening around us, can significantly reduce anxiety, overwhelm and depression. We can relax on every level without tension or stiffness. It can help us to stop the busyness and the distractions in which we are constantly involved. Being an activist from this essence prevents exhaustion and burnout. When I visited the Nobel Prize Museum in Stockholm, I was deeply affected by all the winners, especially the Peace Prize activists who have achieved so much for peace in the world. Most of them, I believe, would have access to the peace essence.

With regular experience of, and access to, the peace essence comes the realisation, not on the level of mind or belief but from within the depth of our being, that peace is all pervading, it needs no external evidence or proof from a secondary source. We become peace personified, we remain non-reactive and calm, we can act and impact the world from this depth. We find ourselves being peaceful in all situations, feeling interconnection, rather than separation. Our responses flow from a conscious, calm alertness, skilful and appropriate to any context of situation.

The aligned Chalice Well Essence is Pacem which "offers the gift of peace to our minds and being."

Trust

The trust essence is an important antidote to a chaotic world because it enables us to truly trust the universe, human nature and life in general as benign and loving, always wanting the best for us, whatever horrible things may be happening. The trust essence assists us to know that we are being taken care of through whatever happens in our lives, positively or negatively. We have a sense of safety and security intrinsic to everything we are and do. This helps us to stop worrying, and our anxieties dissolve. We no longer live our lives defensively and we are able to take risks, explore and remain in a deep, abiding trust.

The common understanding of trust is the belief that someone is good and honest and will not harm you or that you can be certain that someone or something is safe and reliable. If we have low trust, we can become suspicious. As a result, everyone and everything gains the potential to disappoint, take advantage of or harm us. We can access trust essence to a greater or lesser extent depending on the kinds of experience we have had through life. Have people harmed you or let you down? Were your early caretakers reliable or erratic? Is your life safe and predictable or chaotic? Can you commit in your relationships, or do you need a high level of defence and autonomy to feel safe? In many different spheres, including relationships, leadership and mediation, high trust is a component that can make a positive difference to connection and heathy behaviour between people.

Activists may struggle to access the trust essence more than any of the other essences. We often become activists out of being or seeing others, oppressed, dismissed and treated unjustly. Many of us, including me, have serious issues with abuse of authority and power. I have had to work hard on my anti-authority issues and have held many formal positions of authority, yet I have always identified as being a rebel against all forms of abuse of power. I write extensively on different forms of power in my *Goddess Luminary Leadership Wheel* book (Sedgmore 2021).

One of the most profound teachings I have ever experienced is from Almaas on "basic trust," a term he coined to describe how through being in presence we can attune to and live from a deep and profound trust. An experience of basic trust, or the trust essence, cuts through any sense of existing as a separate and isolated individual. Essence trust is not defined through our constructed personality. The trust essence gives us complete confidence to trust in staying completely with whatever we are experiencing in the present moment, without any judgement or preference.

It took a lot of presence for me to learn how to trust. Experiences of presence catapulted me into a whole new level of trust in the universe. I learnt it first through my head, until one of my most powerful experiences of presence enabled a shift into trust which pervaded my whole nervous system. All need for control vanished within an overwhelming sense of trust transfusing my whole body. I was unlimited and expansive with a knowing of total safety and freedom. This experience is constantly with me, in quiet times and amid my actions in the world.

I now live from an intrinsic response to others through the trust essence. Even if I am let down, attacked or betrayed by someone, my basic trust remains. It may hurt me and cause some personal suffering and difficult emotions in my initial reaction, yet the trust remains. Trust has also influenced my relationship to power; I now use power with, for and through people rather than over them. In my personal life I have been blessed with long-term, committed relationships steeped in high trust. In the professional domain I have worked extensively with trust, especially as a leader. Trust has been critical in my activism. I learnt to let go of familiar ways of control and adopted new ways of influencing and protesting through empowerment and resonant relationships. Through collective trust in teams and activist movements, we have achieved outcomes that seemed impossible and difficult. Extinction Rebellion co-creates liberating, peer structures built on trust rather than hierarchy. Trust is at the heart of healthy relationships in every sphere of our lives.

The aligned Chalice Well Essence is Beech which "increases faith, trust and belief that you can and will achieve what you hope for."

Strength

Strength essence is a strong energy that gives us the capacity to withstand a great deal of pressure, stress, anxiety and challenge. It has a feisty and fiery quality that prevents us from being crushed by all the difficult things we must face in the world today. Strength essence gives us a quality of forcefulness and an "I can do" attitude. We become blessed with initiative and courage.

When I feel the strength essence arising, my experience is of my whole body pulsing. It feels alive, dynamic, vibrant and capable. A deep, can-do capacity to get things done enables me, with others, to make a difference for the better.

This is one of the essences that really helps with the toughness and hardness of the world. It stops us from feeling overwhelmed and giving up. It is different than resilience, as it ensures we don't get knocked down or knocked over at all. Strength essence prevents us from ever collapsing or feeling defeated, whereas resilience gives us a bounce-back energy, letting us address any collapse and overwhelm we may have experienced. In strength, we find the energy to do whatever it is we need to do, and we don't feel tired or worn out. There seems to be a constant, ever-flowing fountain of energy available to us. If necessary we can stand on our own, be independent, autonomous, and capable, without any hubris.

Activists need the strength essence to counter the might and dominance of self-interested, fossil fuel corporates, undemocratic governments, unfair justice systems, and inappropriate yielding of power. They need strength to keep challenging and speaking out against all the odds and resistances they continually face. True strength gives a non-narcissistic bigness, stability and power to individuals and activists.

The strength essence enables us to have the energy, fire, initiative and courage to go after our hearts' desire, to fight injustice and to know we can stay the course, however long it takes. We know determination as a solid steadfastness of will, and even if we lose some of the campaigns, we stay strong and keep going, over and over.

One of my favourite activists is Indra Donfrancesco. I admire her enormously. She is five feet tall and petite; I mention this only because it is relevant. This woman's activist superpower is to stand in front of large machinery, especially bulldozers, and make them stop. I have heard her describe her ability to simply stand still and firm as these machines drive towards her, without moving, however close they come. And it works, she stops them, maybe only temporarily. I think the most important learning here is her expression of strength. I believe she is drawing simultaneously on the peace, trust and strength essences. In talks she has given to my students, she describes being totally present and fearless, yet full of courage, peace and strength, she literally faces down a huge machine that could harm her yet never has.

The aligned Chalice Well Essence is Oak which "offers endurance, courage and resilience in the face of life's struggles."

Resilience

The climate and ecological crises are presenting everyday challenges and unexpected or traumatic events that can affect people deeply and can have a lasting impact. People respond to change and trauma differently. The way someone adapts to and recovers from life-changing events and stressful situations is related to their levels of resilience.

Resilience is the process of adapting well in the face of adversity, trauma, tragedy, threats or a significant source of stress. Becoming more resilient helps get us through difficult circumstances, recover and bounce back. It can also involve profound personal growth, and it can bring new insights to improve our life. Being resilient does not mean that we don't experience difficulties or suffering; it can be the difficulties that help us develop the capacity to access the resilience essence. Experiencing resilience essence can change behaviours, thoughts and actions, and it can drastically reduce anxiety or stress responses. We can learn to recognise, reduce or transform reactive tendencies at their inception, thereby stopping them from overwhelming us, giving tremendous inner resilience. I have been fortunate to have easy access to high resilience and have worked closely with many people to help them foster their own resilience.

Resilience is so needed in the world today; it has become a desirable, core quality or competence across many different disciplines. There are many understandings of resilience, as it is so significant in these challenging times.

In ecology, resilience is seen as the ability of a system to absorb disturbance and retain its basic function and structure. We can apply that definition to ourselves as well as to our planet. Jem Bendell, in his seminal paper *Deep Adaptation: A Map for Navigating Climate Tragedy* (2020)[17], defines resilience in the face of climate change and extinction as "what we most value, what we want to keep, and how we keep it."

Resilience gives us the capacity to adapt to short-term challenges, disruptions and changes over the longer term. This is exactly what activists need. When resilient, we can stay in our equanimity through retaining our authenticity and sense of presence. Presence enables our nervous systems to be more resilient and allows them to adapt and respond effectively.

Out of the vast literature and teachings about being calm and resilient, I like the work of Wendy Palmer. She combines the martial art of aikido with mindfulness practice and presence. She proposes a clear connection between an individual's resilience and their ability to live well in stressful and complex environments. She offers techniques that help us become more resilient through recognising how our minds and bodies habitually react to pressure. In stressful situations, often our bodies constrict and they become agitated or reactive. She offers three premises:

1. The body takes a shape before the mind consciously identifies a thought or feeling.
2. Our physical being is the most direct point of intervention.
3. How you sit and stand will change the way you think and speak.

I recommend her book, co-authored with Janet Crawford, *Leadership Embodiment: How the Way We Sit and Stand Can Change the Way We Think and Speak* (2013). It is full of powerful exercises and insights. I also suggest watching her video, "Introducing Leadership Embodiment."[18]

One of the innovative things about Extinction Rebellion is their understanding of how activists frequently burn out, sometimes because their activism is fueled by anger and outrage. Extinction Rebellion holds workshops, trainings, discussions and support groups to improve the resilience of all their rebels.

With the continual increase in conflicts and natural catastrophic events, both urban and rural communities need to increase their resilience. This will be assisted by individuals and activists who can access the resilience essence.

A useful book by Ma'ikwe Ludwig is *Together Resilient: Building Community in the Age of Climate Disruption* (2017). She argues that the best way to create resilience is to build strong local communities. I fully agree; I am involved in a number of resilience projects in my local community of Glastonbury.

The aligned Chalice Well Essence is Oak which "offers endurance, courage and resilience in the face of life's struggles."

Love

In the love essence we experience a positive, benign, nurturing and optimising experience of open heartedness and compassion. We move towards and receive others with a sense of embracing, sweetness, softness and gentleness. Our hearts overflow with kindness, compassion, contentment, and a deep, abiding, selfless love. The love essence holds and soothes like a cradling of the most exquisite kind. We soften and open within a melting that feels beautiful, warm and cosy. We feel held and safe. We know viscerally that love is the benign fabric of the universe, goodness itself. When the love essence is fully expressed it feels unconditional; we become love itself, and everything is love. Love feels boundless, abundant and readily available, with a freedom of heart unconstrained by our personality. It brings the capacity and intrinsic desire to live a loving, good and virtuous life, for its own sake, not out of fear or a need for reward.

I have explored love in all its shapes and expressions and I do my best to live from love, from a deep, unconditional and authentic love that can be tough, fierce and challenging as well as kind, embracing, expansive and empowering. I have fallen in romantic love many times and have been very fortunate to experience unconditional mother, grandmother and stepmom love.

For me, my activism is love made visible. My professional work, service and activism have always been an offering of love, through service, into the world. I adore fostering the potential and brilliance of others as well as challenging injustice and oppression. I love the world enough to stand up and speak my authentic truth, however hard that may be at times.

An excellent book on love is *All About Love: New Visions* by bell hooks (2001). This is a powerful exploration of how to love in a society that doesn't encourage the deeper levels of connection and intimacy possible. When the love essence arises, all forms of love, connection and intimacy are possible.

Our emotions can obscure presence. It is important not to push our emotions away and to feel deeply whichever emotion we are feeling without acting it out. If we feel, access, penetrate, allow, acknowledge, dis-identify and get in touch with the full range of our emotions, then let them go, we will no longer disconnect from presence. We will move beyond the grip and confusion of emotionality to feel directly the love essence.

It helps to keep our hearts as open as possible and to respond to everyone, and every situation, with love and compassion. It is easy for our personality to think it can own or control love while feeling fear, upset and suffering as well as nice and warm feelings. Often the issue of vulnerability arises when we try to be open and expansive, and we may be caught in projecting our emotions onto others. When discharging emotions onto another person, we prevent essence from moving through us.

In my workplace I first used the word love overtly in 1990, as a senior leader, when I was dean of Croydon Business School. Half the staff were appalled, and my deputies advised me to stop using it. I was only thirty-five, new in post and surrounded by men, so I did stop—it felt too scary. By 1998, I had gained sufficient confidence, so when I was appointed as the new principal of Guildford College and we cocreated a new college vision and values, it had the word love in it, within the phrase "love of learning." Yes, it was somewhat tempered. I am delighted that in the 2020s it is not uncommon to hear the word love openly mentioned in leadership and organisations.

I have expressed love as an activist through my commitment to and actions on diversity and inclusion, by proactively encouraging others to bring their whole, fullest, unique selves into their professional work. My favourite expression of love is within my family and through cocreating a loving culture in the communities and organisations I belong to:spaces in which differences, as well as similarities are truly celebrated and respected.

I love this beautiful quote from Dr. Martin Luther King who named his activist movement "beloved community": "When I speak of love I am not speaking of some sentimental and weak response which is little more than emotional bosh. Love is the supreme unifying principle of life. It is somehow the key that unlocks the door which leads to ultimate reality."

The aligned Chalice Well Essence is Blend of Roses which "offers tenderness and unconditional love."

Flow

Flow can happen spontaneously or through consciously developing it; with practice it becomes more continuous. Flow is an experience of everything moving smoothly and naturally, with ease. Flow essence generates fulfilment and enjoyment as every action follows naturally and easily from the previous one. Our skills and being function at their optimal levels. Some people experience flow when they are completely involved in an activity that feels timeless. We know when we are acting in flow.

Flow can be a transpersonal experience and can also be very useful and practical in our everyday lives. Flow can happen when engrossed in almost any activity: reading, meditating, dancing, running, during our favourite sport or when playing a musical instrument. When we are in flow, we forget the world around us and become totally focused on the current action we are engaged in. We may not notice time passing, and we may even feel we are in a dimension of non-linear time. We may have no notion of how long we may have been doing something. An hour may seem like three seconds as time loses any relevance or importance.

Flow frees the mind of mental clutter or busyness, and we know exactly what to do without worrying or anxiety. We are infused with a feeling of ease with no difficulty, blockage or need to strain or make conscious effort. We notice an absence of anxiety and burnout.

Being aware of whether we are "pushing against" or "flowing with" is important. The flow essence is not the same thing as "go with the flow." Go with the flow can mean giving up and going passively with what is happening, even something that is not in alignment with our highest emerging potential.

"Flowing with" is an engaged and proactive process which requires sensing into the moment and into a bigger, more expansive potential waiting to unfold. We organically partner with that emerging potential and allow the flow of what wants to happen in service of something bigger. This can include all aspects of our activism.

One way of expressing flow is that we are no longer dancing: we are the dance (or running or singing or doing a work task). We are doing from a place of non-doing. Wu Wei is the Taoist principle of non-doing, not forcing, or effortless action. It can only be experienced beyond the thinking mind. Effortless activism is being in a state of flow. In Wu Wei there is no effort involved by the cognitive mind and there is no striving involved. The feeling is one of effortlessness and spontaneity, and it can even seem as if there is no one doing anything. True Wu Wei does not mean doing nothing. It is developing an inner non-resistance and surrender to the flow of each moment. From here, we respond appropriately to whatever the situation requires.

Satish Kumar, an environmental activist interviewed in *Talking the Walk* by Brian Draper (2013),[19] describes the experience of flow as an activist in his beautiful words: "My activism is not contrived, not planned; it comes as naturally to me as breathing, and I think I am going to serve the world, and the earth, as an activist until the last breath of my life because it has become part of me. And I am not looking for any achievement, any outcome: what I am doing has its own, intrinsic rightness. I do what I feel is right for me. And that is all it is."

The aligned Chalice Well Essence is Essene which assists us to "reconnect in order to experience more harmony and flow with the rhythm of life."

Presence Essences and Activism

The Presence Essences are the qualities that help us to cultivate the profound expression of the best we can be. They support us in becoming skilful Presence Activists, constantly acting and serving from presence. Activism from one or more of the essences supports our capacity to act from our highest potential, acting skilfully amidst the challenges and seductions of climate peril. They also reduce and dissolve our anxiety. Presence relaxes our urgency instinct, reduces unhelpful catastrophising and enables appropriate and skilful responses to pertinent issues.

For me, the highest form of activism is all the essences made visible through how we act in the world. I summarise below, one by one, what each essence contributes.

Strength gives us a "can do" capacity to get things done and to make a difference in the world. Resilience enables us to keep going through tough challenges and to keep bouncing back. Joy enables us to remember how wonderful it is just to be alive and fills us with gratitude. Trust brings wise guidance from a deep source through which we discern which actions are best to engage in for the greater good. Peace gives us equanimity and a profound knowing that all is well, and always will be, however difficult the situation or suffering. Flow supports our activism to flow easefully and creatively through us. Activism is love made visible, love for our planet, all species and ourselves, as we work to save Mother Earth from the harm and destruction she is facing.

The seven Presence Essences can arise individually or as several together according to what is needed in any particular situation, relationship or context. As we understand, practice becomes more proficient when we access presence through the Presence Flower. Thus the more we will be able to access the essences that are needed in every moment. The more present we are the more easily they will arise.

When all essences are available to us, there is no burnout, collapse or anxiety, only an appropriate and skilful rising and response to every challenge or opportunity that comes our way. When we drop out of presence, we may forget how spacious, benign, beautiful, precious and capable we are. The essences are far more healing, benign and calming than our usual personality preoccupations.

I encourage you to explore and experiment with these seven Presence Essences in your activism and in your life. Some of them may be more elusive or difficult to access than others. The more we reside directly, fully and viscerally in presence, the more we will be able to access all of them.

***

I hope you resonate with the Presence Flower, especially the Presence Essences. The other layers and petals of the Flower are shared in Chapters 7 and 8. We now move into an exploration of climate anxiety and my Anxiety Flower in the next chapter.

Chapter 4

Presence and Climate Anxiety

***

"If you want to conquer the anxiety of life, live in the moment."
Amit Ray

***

Introduction

Climate anxiety does not yet receive the attention it deserves within our society. In 2019 Oxford Languages[20] made climate emergency the word of the year and reported a 4,290% increase in the use of the term "eco-anxiety" compared with the year before. I view climate anxiety as an inevitability in the face of the threat of climate and ecological peril, rather than a distorted pathology, deficit or disorder. It affects everyone alive today to a greater or lesser extent. In these current times, anxiety has a rational place. Being anxious about the climate and ecological crisis is a reasonable and understandable response to a genuinely dangerous situation.

Anxiety is problematic when it becomes so strong or overwhelming that we are unable to live a functional life and to cope with daily living. Anyone experiencing extreme or debilitating climate anxiety should have this taken seriously and be able to obtain appropriate support to cope with it. The capacity to cope with climate change, to calm all forms of anxiety—especially climate anxiety—to increase resilience, to enable healthy choices and to take conscious action is needed now, more than ever before.

I draw on presence to manage my own anxiety and to remain centred and calm amidst the stressful knowing that our planet is being damaged beyond repair. The acute need to deal with climate peril, disappearing biodiversity, extinction and human distress is obvious, yet the incompetence and reluctance of patriarchy and capitalism to solve the issue is very real.

Elin Kelsey, in *Hope Matters: Why Changing the Way We Think Is Critical to Solving the Environmental Crisis* (2020), describes how our emotional responses and concerns about the environment affect us in numerous ways. This may involve keeping us awake at night, feeling the pain of seeing the destruction we will leave to future generations, choosing not to have children, feeling anxious and grieving for the world we are destroying.

Every time we watch the news, read a newspaper or go onto social media, we see something distressing. It is difficult to avoid the bombardment of horrific images documenting the impact of extreme weather, war damage and natural disasters. We are shown constantly how animals, sea life, vegetation and humans are dying or displaced from their environment. In addition, we may have been personally impacted by an aspect of climate peril crashing into our own lives. Our homes may have been flooded, our local air may be filled with smoke from burning fires or traffic pollution, our house may have collapsed due to intense hurricanes, flooding, volcanic eruptions, tsunamis or earthquakes. The ongoing destruction of our planet inevitably affects us. Living in rural England, I am shielded from the worst effects. On my travels in Canada, however, I have witnessed the devastating effect of forest fires close up. Friends overseas have lost homes to fires, floods and earthquakes.

The *Nurturing the Fields of Change* report published by the Alef Trust in 2023,[21] focuses on the "inner dimensions of the crises we have been experiencing." They recognise that "our global challenges are rooted in dysfunctional mental states and social dynamics, and that we need to engage in inner work to evolve our capacities and skills in addressing world-wide insecurities and volatilities." All the political, economic, technological and environmental aspects of climate peril need to be challenged by climate activists, yet without internal resilience, equanimity and skilfulness, activists will become exhausted in the face of the massive task involved.

***

I have had struggles with being able to face the climate peril without denial or anxiety. I can get caught in a loop of thinking about the dreadful world my granddaughters and great nephews and nieces might have to live in. When I am with them, I see their innocence and aliveness, and I become filled with concern for their future. I feel the grief rising, allow it, breathe deeply, sense into my body, feel the sensations and move into presence. The joy essence returns, and I stay with enjoying the time I have with them in that very moment. The days when we could definitely bring about a better future for our children have gone. As a Western baby boomer, I feel that my generation is the luckiest alive. We have benefited from owning our own home, good pensions, free education and abundant employment opportunities. My two granddaughters at ages seventeen and twenty face so many difficult issues, far worse than my generation.

What Is Climate Anxiety?

Climate anxiety is a mixture of psychological, physiological, emotional and physical effects generated by the direct or perceived impact of climate peril. It is becoming a recognised diagnosis, as it is so prevalent. If we care about our planet and keep up to date on climate and ecological issues, then some level of anxiety is inevitable. It is a rational, sensible and appropriate response to what we are all facing.

Climate anxiety includes a wide range of feelings and symptoms, including grief, tension, overwhelm, burnout, fear, suspicion, defeat and stuckness generated by having to face the potential disastrous consequences facing us, and the planet.

Anxiety, of any kind, is a state of negative expectation and a response to danger, whether real or imagined. It is characterised by increased arousal and apprehension which turns into distressing states and symptoms.

Dahr Jamail describes poignantly his suffering and climate anxiety in *Grieving My Way into Loving the Planet* (2020) when he writes:

> My heart was broken open by both the magnificent beauty and power in each place… as well as how quickly it was all being lost. Standing on bare ground in Alaska once covered by two hundred feet of ice from the Byron Glacier where I used to go climbing felt like a gut punch. Snorkeling atop the Great Barrier Reef bleached white and dying from overheated ocean waters, I found my mask filling up with my tears. Each field trip broke my heart open with awe and sadness, time and time again… I was reminded… that a broken heart can hold the entire universe.

Climate anxiety isn't necessarily caused by pre-existing conditions of anxiety, although there may be a correlation with them. As a survival response to the inevitable dangers of the climate crisis, it can arise suddenly and unexpectedly and affect you for short or long periods. An important aspect of anxiety is the anticipation involved, as it is future-focused. We can feel anxiety for things that have not yet happened, and that we anticipate or catastrophise may happen. When anxious, we wait for the next disaster to happen and may become immobilised and stuck, unable to make decisions in case our choice turns out to be the wrong one. We may also overthink everything, fill our head with worst case scenarios and feel huge immobilising fear.

Other terms are being used to explore the various impacts of climate peril. These include climate environmental trauma, climate distress, eco-distress, anticipatory grief, global dread, ecological anxiety, disaster mental health, apocalypse fatigue, solastalgia and eco-grief.

Glenn Albrecht, an eco-philosopher, has coined the term solastalgia, a combination of the Latin word for comfort (solacium) and the Greek root for pain (algia). His new word captures the existential and psychological homesickness people feel when their environment undergoes irreversible change or degradation and is no longer felt as a place of safety. Two powerful books exploring solastalgia and how to repair and heal a solastalgia-damaged psyche are Paul Bogard's *Solastalgia: An Anthology of Emotion in a Disappearing World* (2023), and Glenn Albrecht's *Earth Emotions: New Words for a New World* (2019).

Symptoms of Anxiety

When we are anxious, our nervous systems are constantly jangled. We may feel mentally and physically unwell, and our energy feels low and unavailable. When our body is constantly on high alert and remains flooded with stress chemicals, we develop problems such as foggy thinking, mood fluctuations, exhaustion, meltdowns, over-reacting, high blood pressure, heart issues, immune illnesses, digestive sensitivity, overeating, headaches, nausea and difficulty sleeping, as well as anxiety. Our bodies are not designed to live in a constant state of anxiety. Panic attacks illustrate the spontaneous arising of anxiety. They involve sudden periods of intense fear and discomfort that are distressing and debilitating. They can manifest through palpitations, sweating, chest pain, chest discomfort, shortness of breath, trembling, dizziness, numbness and confusion. They may also be accompanied by feelings of impending doom or of losing control. The duration of symptoms can last seconds, half an hour or several hours. Fortunately, panic attacks, while deeply distressing, are not physically dangerous or life threatening.

All the symptoms listed above create chaos in your sympathetic nervous system, causing the body to feel it is in danger. A high level of stress or anxiety keeps our heart rates elevated, dilates pupils, raises blood pressure and keeps everything in our body on high alert.

Some peoples' nervous systems are more robust than others. You may have a highly sensitive nervous system that is stimulated and very easily triggered. Common triggers include loud noises, bright lights, strong smells, crowds of people, texture, being alone and trauma re-stimulation: things that are not a serious threat to survival yet affect us as if they were. It is important to identify your triggers so you can avoid or reduce them to lessen the severity of your symptoms.

We all cope differently and while focussing on climate peril may cause overwhelming anxiety for some, others may be able to face it head on. If we only associate climate peril with uncontrollable disaster it will affect our brains and our nervous systems negatively. Too much overwhelm reduces our motivation to act. If your energy feels drained, your nervous system over stimulated, your emotions pulled in competing directions, then it is important to find a way of anchoring, grounding yourself, amidst all these exhausting demands.

Anouchka Grose in her book *A Guide to Eco-Anxiety: How to Protect the Planet and Your Mental Health* (2020) explores a second meaning of the word anxious, which is "eagerness to do something." This definition is more energetic and contains the possibility of being able to act. This definition involves anticipation of wanting to take action and to contribute something useful. Each of us can determine what is right for us to do, both individually and collectively. Doing nothing is also a choice.

You and Climate Anxiety

For many years I was in denial about my own levels of anxiety, especially climate anxiety, keeping it suppressed with overeating and staying busy. I am interested in what climate anxiety means for you, and I offer a few questions for reflection.

What arises for you when you ponder and reflect upon the two words "climate anxiety"? Is it something of which you have direct experience? How much does it overwhelm you, or not? Have you gone deep into the causes? What are you doing to alleviate your climate anxiety? How might you be suppressing your anxiety? What different forms of coping with climate anxiety have you tried? Do your friends and family have climate anxiety? When any anxiety arises in you, how do you dispel or manage it? What experience do you have of presence helping you with your climate anxiety?

You may wish to explore the Climate Change Anxiety Scale by emerge. This is a 22-item measure of emotional response to climate change. The measure has four sub-scales including cognitive and emotional impairment, functional impairment, personal experience of climate change and behavioural engagement. The scale has been validated in the US.[22]

The Climate Anxiety Scale (CAS) by Frontiers is a thirteen-item questionnaire for assessing climate anxiety (CA) as a psychological response to climate change. The CAS consists of two sub-scales, namely, cognitive impairment and functional impairment.[23]

Sarah Ray offers useful resources in her book *A Field Guide to Climate Anxiety: How to Keep Your Cool on a Warming Planet* (2020). She draws on her work as a teacher in the US to offer support to the climate generation through her "effective arc of environmental studies curricula." She focuses on emotional reactions to climate peril, as she believes it is just as important for her students to learn how to address their feelings as it is for them to learn about environmental disruption and injustice. I totally agree. I recommend her book to complement mine, as she dives deeper into emotional intelligence, something I have already written and taught about in my own book (2021).

The Scale of the Issue

Climate anxiety, experienced by millions of people, is a growing concern among people of all ages. It is a global and systemic issue, as well as an individual experience. Chronic fear of environmental catastrophe is affecting many young people's daily lives, with six in ten feeling very worried about the climate crisis, as reported in the Guardian newspaper article by Andrew Gregory, "'Eco-anxiety': fear of environmental doom weighs on young people" (2021).[24] He describes the results of a 2021 international survey of climate anxiety in young people aged sixteen to twenty-five, which showed that the psychological burdens of climate crisis were "profoundly affecting huge numbers of these young people around the world." The research also offers insights into how young people's emotions were linked to their feelings of betrayal and abandonment caused by governments and adults. Governments were seen as failing to respond adequately, leaving young people with "no future" and leaving "humanity doomed."

Another piece of research that evidences how climate anxiety is rapidly growing includes the University of Bath results of its 2023 *Climate Action Survey* of nearly 5,000 respondents. Their research illustrated that 19% of students and 25% of staff said they were "extremely worried" about climate change, while 36% and 33% stated they were "very worried." Climate worry was higher in 2023 than in 2022.[25]

According to a 2020 survey, *Stress in America, A National Mental Health Crisis,* out of 3,000 U.S. residents polled by the American Psychological Association, 60% of participants reported feeling overwhelmed by the number of issues that America is currently facing.[26]

In 2021, a global survey in ten countries, "Climate anxiety in children and young people and their beliefs about government responses to climate change: a global survey," explored how children and young people felt about climate change. They found high levels of anxiety as the 10,000 participants reported feelings of sadness, anxiety, anger, powerlessness, helplessness and guilt.[27]

I am particularly concerned about young people. In my conversations with them, they express a general sense of hopelessness from living with climate anxiety, with a constant tension of feeling that everything is ultimately hopeless. They want to be hopeful because giving up and feeling overwhelmed makes their anxiety worse. Many young people are so immobilised by their anxiety that they are unable to act. Others have become full time climate activists and alleviate their anxiety through action, protests and trying to make a difference. Being well-informed about climate peril and its potential impacts can help some people to reduce their anxiety by providing a sense of empowerment and choice. Part of climate anxiety can be feeling misunderstood or unacknowledged by society or the people around you—when nobody else seems to notice this urgent issue in the same way as you.

Joining a support group or finding people who see things as you do can be of huge benefit. I also think that inter-generational communication about climate peril is really important. I have learnt to work through, cope with and articulate my climate anxiety so that I can help my grandchildren and hopefully others, especially young people, to cope with their anxiety.

Presence as an Antidote to Climate Anxiety

The Presence Flower is a profound process to dissolve anxiety and to free us up mentally, emotionally and physically. When we partner the Anxiety Flower with the Presence Flower, we can honour and accept all the anxiety energies while knowing that they can alleviate and dissolve. Through presence we can gain, or regain, the ability to act and feel agency, to be an effective and skilful activist.

When we are in presence we breathe more slowly and deeply. As we relax and our breath slows, our bodies and nervous systems calm and relax as practicing presence brings our sensory and neurological input to a minimum. We can listen and respond to our physical, physiological and emotional needs.

Practising presence directly affects our brains and nervous systems in positive ways. As our sympathetic and parasympathetic autonomic nervous systems regulate, we move out of stress and high alert. Presence calms the amygdala part of our brain, the part that manages our instincts and survival. If notions of the brain and nervous system are new to you, I offer Appendix II for brief information on *The Physiology of Calming Our Nervous System and Brain*.

Presence is the primary way I manage, relax and calm my anxiety and my nervous system in the face of climate peril. Presence also helps me to rest and restore. I manage my anxiety from within rather than being dependent on external sources, addictions or other people. It has not been a quick, overnight cure, but rather more of a gradual, long lasting, internal, self-generating and profound solution. Presence has literally dissolved my anxiety, as I have learned to access the seven Presence Essences more continuously. Through presence, I can face the terrible things that are happening and allow the anxiety energies to arise, and then, without acting them out, I am able to move through and beyond them. This is because I have more space and capacity to tolerate any anxiety energies arising. I notice them, remain non-attached, move into one or more of the

Presence Portals and allow the Presence Essence(s) to arise. As the essences shift into being my centre of gravity, I can be more than just my personality; with less reactivity, my anxiety has less and less impact. I am now more grounded and stable in the presence essences rather than anxiety. I have turned my anxiety and personality dissolving into a healing journey.

Presence enables us to have equanimity, to gain balance and insight. We can tolerate any internal commentaries and anxieties that still run inside us. We experience greater freedom to pause and make conscious choices. We put an end to any behaviours that no longer serve us or anyone else. The only long-lasting, deep, profound change is through presence as an antidote to anxiety.

In addition to presencing, I have also undertaken three complementary ways of understanding and reducing my anxiety. The first consists of understanding and deconstructing my personality through therapy and significant shadow work. Secondly, I have constantly inquired into and reflected on my behaviours, emotional intelligence, motivations and impact on others. I have found the Enneagram the most useful self-awareness tool. Thirdly, a wide range of spiritual rituals and practices have been crucial in helping me understand my anxiety. I am intrigued by the work of Andrew Newberg and his findings in *How God Changes Your Brain: Breakthrough Findings from a Leading Neuroscientist* (2010). With Mark Walkman, he discovered that if you take out the religious and spiritual aspects of ritual and spiritual practices, including any notion or belief in God, they still have the same effect on our brains. This is because presencing activities and practices strengthen neural functioning in parts of the brain that lower anxiety and buffer us from stress. A fascinating finding from their work is that "deep yawning" will physiologically relax you in less than a minute and will allow you to move rapidly into a presence state.

New alliances are growing between psychology and activism to help alleviate climate anxiety, as described in a powerful book *Holding the Hope: Reviving Psychological and Spiritual Agency in the Face of Climate Change* (Linda Ashley et al., 2023). This collection of essays explores how to grapple with anxiety and hope in these challenging times. It is edited by members of the Climate Psychology Alliance and the Climate and Environmental Emergency Coaching Alliance, two groups who accept and are responding to the psychological and spiritual needs of people deeply suffering due to the climate emergency. It blends psychotherapeutic, spiritual approaches and indigenous wisdom, and discusses radical hope, active, hope, rewilding hope, and different ways of holding hope. They recommend going deep into "the solid ground, common ground, the ground of connection and cooperation, from which we can find relief and joy." Their perspective is similar to mine: that finding the ground, presence, enables people to cope with whatever they are facing, especially anxiety.

I encourage you to explore complementary approaches to assist you in calming and reducing your anxiety until you can be sufficiently in presence to dissolve it completely. There are numerous psychotherapeutic approaches including Cognitive Behavioural Therapy (CBT) and Acceptance and commitment therapy (ACT). Finding a support group might be invaluable. Simple things like getting enough sleep and looking after yourself through exercise, deep breathing, massage, a healthy diet, relaxation, journaling and spending time in nature can help considerably. When we are consumed with negative projections or pessimism, we are not living in the moment, so remaining in a state of presence, in the now, keeps us calm enough to prevent or dissolve any anxiety symptoms.

Anxiety Flower Overview

The Anxiety Flower, figure 2 below, is the counterpart to the Presence Flower. It illustrates the Anxiety Gnosis, portals, energies, impacts and results that can be dissolved, healed and transformed by the Presence Flower and all its layers and petals.

***

Figure 2 Anxiety Flower

The Anxiety Flower assists in understanding, mapping and working through different aspects of anxiety. It illustrates all the resistances, reactivities, constrictions and blocked energies that get dissolved when we relax, embody and illuminate through the potency of presence. I have included anxiety energies from other peoples' experiences, as well as my own. Not everyone will experience all of them, yet most of us will have experienced one or more of these at some point in our lives.

To be free from anxiety, we need to identify all our anxious behaviours, thoughts and actions. The Anxiety Flower names and acknowledges the difficult energies, suffering and qualities that need to be dissolved to alleviate our suffering. It comprises Anxiety Gnosis, six Anxiety Portals, seven Anxiety Energies, two Anxiety Impacts and six Anxiety Results.

Anxiety Gnosis (layer 1)

At the centre of the Anxiety Flower is a direct, visceral experience of anxiety—Anxiety Gnosis. The direct and visceral knowing from a deep, profound, subjective, personal suffering that feels palpably real.

Anxiety Portals (layer 5)

I explore these second, as they are key to knowing how we close down and block presence when we experience Anxiety. The six anxiety portals block any journeying or transition into presence. We feel deeply disconnected and alienated.

Constricted

Closed

Numbed

Surfacing

Unconscious

Judgemental

Anxiety Energies (layer 3)

The seven Anxiety Energies are powerful energies which block us from experiencing and knowing our deepest nature. We are consumed with anxiety and suffer deeply when trapped in these energies. We dissolve these through experience of the Presence Essences.

Grief

Tension

Suspicion

Defeat

Overwhelm

Fear

Stuckness

Anxiety Impacts (layer 2)

The two Anxiety Impacts of Immobilised and Denial occur when we are consumed by the anxiety energies and stop experiencing presence. These two impacts stifle and constrict our inner and outer worlds. Immobilised literally stops us moving, and we retreat from the world into isolation. Denial makes us disconnected and out of touch with what is really happening around us.

Immobilised

Denial

Anxiety Results (layer 4)

When we are impacted by Anxiety on a regular or constant basis, we feel disconnected and suffer significantly. The six Results are directly linked to the Impacts. Immobilised and Denial foster three Results each.

Self-Interest
Burnout
Unhealthy Relationships

***

Separation
Inner Critic
Shadow Personality

Anxiety Gnosis

At the centre of the Anxiety Flower is Anxiety Gnosis: the somatic, mental and visceral knowing of anxiety through direct experience. We are not able to be calm and present when our physical, mental, emotional, psychological and nervous systems become overwhelmed and dysregulated. Our minds feel worn out or are constantly churning. Our hearts feel closed, as we need to protect ourselves from the emotional overload we are encountering. We can feel immobilised and unable to find any meaning, purpose or satisfaction in our lives. We may feel like hiding under the duvet, unable to find meaning. Looking at a beautiful flower or landscape in nature can lead us to thoughts of planetary devastation and the annihilation.

For many of us, Anxiety Gnosis is not something that we can turn on or off by choice or at will. It can be triggered by a particular event or appear spontaneously for no apparent reason.

Instead of knowing our Presence Gnosis at our centre, there is anxiety. Instead of interconnection we see separation between ourselves and everything else, seeing only differences, creating walls and conflict instead of harmony. Instead of being expansive through and illuminated we experience the negative, blocked energies of the essences. When in presence Anxiety Gnosis is dissolved by Presence Gnosis.

Anxiety Portals

When we are anxious each of the Presence Portals becomes more difficult to access. They are the opposite experience of the Presence Portals.

When in presence, Constricted is dissolved by Relaxing, Closed is dissolved by Opening, Numbed is dissolved by Sensing, Surfacing is dissolved by Deepening, Unconscious is dissolved by Observing and Judgemental is dissolved by Allowing.

Constricted

Instead of Relaxing all aspects of our heads, heart and body, we tighten and Constrict them. Our bodies may begin to ache and distract us from being in presence. We cannot think clearly or creatively. Our hearts' space feels defended and inaccessible.

Closed

Instead of Opening our hearts and minds, everything feels Closed, including our body. We feel cut off from all the Presence Portals and unable to open to presence at all.

Numbed

Numbed describes a feeling of being emotionally and physically unresponsive. In this state we are unable to feel or experience presence. When physically numb, you cannot feel or think anything; you feel blank. This blocks any sensitivity and awareness to Sensing what is happening internally or externally.

Surfacing

While we are Surfacing, we remain at a superficial level of our thought and emotions, unable to experience Deepening into our inner thoughts, feelings and identity. We skim rather than dive, remaining with the superficial instead of moving into the depth

113

and complexity of knowing and experiencing who we truly are, being in fullest presence.

Unconscious

Instead of being aware and Observing from an inner space of non-attachment, we remain Unconscious and asleep to the nuances and finer aspects of our body, heart and mind as portals into presence. We forget to witness and observe what is happening. We remain ignorant on every level to our deeper intentions, motivations and complexities. When deeply Unconscious, we may not even be able to observe that we are asleep and oblivious.

Judgemental

Instead of Allowing whatever is happening in the moment, we judge who we are, what we are doing and how we are being. We feel the sharpness and pain of being Judgemental about everyone and everything we see, blocking the flow of presence.

Anxiety Energies

The seven Anxiety Energies cover over the Presence Essences described in the Presence Flower. They are grief, tension, suspicion, defeat, overwhelm, fear and stuckness. They are energies formed within our constructed personality that keep us disconnected from presence. Anxiety plays a crucial role in keeping us alert and alive, so it may not be sensible, or feasible to eliminate it completely. We do, however, need to manage our anxiety and maintain it at levels which do not immobilise us. The more frequently we are in presence, the more the Anxiety Energies will be dissolved appropriately by the Presence Essences.

When we are in presence, Grief—the strong feeling of loss and overwhelming sadness—is dissolved by Joy. Overwhelm from all that is happening is dissolved by Resilience. Tensions that generate internal worry and constant thinking are dissolved by Peace. Being Suspicious through mistrusting and doubting everything, especially the climate change science and evidence, is dissolved by Trust. Defeat, in which everything seems impossible and beyond our capability, is dissolved by Strength. The constriction and anxiousness of Fear is dissolved by Love, and the Stuckness of feeling paralysed, stagnant and blocked is dissolved by Flow. I now describe each of the Anxiety Energies in more detail.

Grief

Grief is our emotional response to any form of significant loss. The grief of climate peril can be triggered by learning of the loss of species and feeling that ultimately the whole planet may be destroyed. Ecological grief is the grief felt in relation to experienced or anticipated ecological losses, including the loss of species, ecosystems and meaningful landscapes. A new field of disaster mental health has emerged to respond to the detrimental psychological effects of extreme weather events. For climate grief I think we need both private and public spaces to express our true feelings and the depth of the devastation through which we are going.

Many of us experience a deep grief when we fully comprehend that the future will be worse that what we know now. As a baby boomer, I grieve that my children and grandchildren will have far worse economic, living, work and habitat prospects than I ever had.

It is important to grieve for the suffering of the planet, for the possibility of a dystopian future that we have created and cannot control, for the loss of the dreams we are not able to fulfil, and for the children we may choose not to bring into the world. To be able to live our lives, we must cope, adapt, move through and learn to live with our grief, whatever the nature of the loss.

Grief is a strong feeling of loss and overwhelming sadness, an all-body experience as well as an emotional one. It grips and causes genuine pain which can knock you over in constant waves that feel insurmountable and never ending. The intensity of grief can feel unbearable. We cry a lot, sometimes uncontrollably, with grief. We may go through many different losses throughout our lives. Loss can be physical: losing a loved one, human, animal or close relationship. We can experience the loss of a job, important roles with which we identify, children leaving home or a group within which we experience deep belonging.

As I was writing this book, my ex-husband died unexpectedly. We parted amicably after a seventeen-year relationship and lived different lives for thirty years, as we both happily remarried. We remained friends and kept in touch. I was amazed at the depth of my grief at his passing as he was not in my daily life. I now understand that grief is determined by the depth of the emotional bond formed and the memories made. The presence antidote to grief is joy.

Tension

Climate peril generates tension both within us and between people and nations. Tension within us invokes internal worry and a busy mind that will not stop thinking in different, conflicting directions. Our nervous system is naturally relaxed when there is nothing we worry about. When we become tense everything inside us feels conflicted, running amok with nervous energy, restlessness and hyper vigilance. We are unable to settle on anything, constantly on the move, unable to relax, and we don't really focus on anything; we constantly get distracted and disturbed by the tension of conflicting perspectives and demands. Our internal worry and monkey mind will not stop thinking. Our bodies become more and more stiff, as we literally hold ourselves tensely—a habit that eventually takes a physical toll on our bodies. We may become physically unwell or develop tension headaches which are incredibly debilitating.

We become tight, jumpy and fragile. The horrors of climate peril feel amplified within our physical, emotional and mental faculties to such an extent that we may feel physically ill, unable to cope or unable to face the issues and hardships ahead.

Differences in opinion between us and others may bring relationship tension. It is clear that tensions continue to build between different nations on how they work together, or not, to solve climate peril. The presence antidote to tension is resilience.

Suspicion

When we feel suspicious, we begin to doubt everything, including the climate change science and evidence. We get lost in the huge amount of conflicting evidence available, and it becomes very difficult to trust anyone or anything we are being told, regardless of the perspective from which it originates. We may get caught up in conspiracy theories, accuse scientists of exaggerating and even ridicule anything that does not fit our preconceptions or wishes. An anxious mind easily falls into being suspicious of the abounding information on climate change and the ecological issues all around us. We don't know what, or who, to trust and our minds whirl with doubt, mistrust and confusion. While doubt can take the form of healthy questioning, suspicious doubt has a negative, draining and chronic uncertainly to it. It is painful if we don't know who or what to rely upon, always looking to be disappointed, let down or deliberately misled. The presence antidote to suspicion is trust.

Defeat

For many people, climate anxiety engenders an existential feeling of dread combined with a feeling of being powerless to do anything to shape their future. Climate disasters have increased rates of suicide, depression and anxiety. In defeat we lose all our agency. We feel powerless and unable to act because it feels impossible to achieve, or to do anything. Over time this becomes utterly debilitating. We believe that everything is conspiring to be the worst it can possibly be, so there is no point in trying. Everything seems impossible, negative and awful until nothing can be done about it whatsoever. This is the place where we lose our agency completely. We give up because we feel that whatever we do won't work or won't be good enough. We can feel defeated before we have even tried. The intention and desire to act and make a difference disappears in a fog of everything feeling too much. This can lead us into becoming "climate doomers," someone who believes we have already lost the planet to climate peril, so there is nothing we can do. In defeat, we can fall into a downward spiral without believing in, or offering any, solutions. The presence antidote to defeat is strength.

Overwhelm

In overwhelm, everything feels like it has loaded up and landed on top of us until we have no space left, no capacity to respond. We lose our ability to bounce back, and we literally feel a huge weight and heaviness from all that is happening in and around us. This may cause us to hide under the duvet or stop functioning. Some people describe a sense of drowning or floundering and an inability to cope with the avalanche that has landed on them. We don't feel that we can change or affect anything in our lives or in the world about us.

My friends have shared with me how, when in the grip of climate overwhelm, they overreact to minor incidents, are easily panicked at small things, withdraw and eventually become isolated. They also experience significant mood changes, constant irritability, anxiety and weepiness. They have difficulty concentrating, making decisions and solving problems. In this space they feel unable to change or affect anything about climate peril.

It may help to recognise the normality of feeling overwhelmed by the challenges of changing our current carbon-intensive lifestyles. We can also be overwhelmed by the lack of visible impact of our individual choices on the global scale of peril. This really affects me.

Yet everything we do really matters. Laura van Dernoot Lipsky, in *The Age of Overwhelm: Strategies for the Long Haul* (2018), names our current time as "the age of overwhelm."

Everyone feels overwhelmed at some time in their life when things seem to pile up. What overwhelms one person may not bother someone else. The continuum of overwhelm can range from feeling occasional surges of overwhelm to coming apart at the seams.

I remember two years of overwhelm when my mother-in-law had terminal cancer. That same year I was in a nasty car crash, my daughter was being bullied at school and I intensely disliked my new, demanding job. The culmination of all these things left me exhausted, depleted, deflated and hugely overwhelmed. It took a serious toll on my energy, vitality, mentality and physical health. I struggled to think clearly and rationally. Any issue felt huge, and at times I just felt that it all was too much to sort out. There were days when I felt paralysed and unable to function; even everyday simple tasks felt impossible. It was my presence practice that helped me move through and function. The presence antidote to overwhelm is resilience.

Fear

In fear, we don't feel held or soothed and we experience danger everywhere. We live on red alert, all the time expecting to be harmed, betrayed or treated badly. This is the place that we can catastrophise and see everything through the worst possible lens. We worry, we feel agitated, we cannot relax and our nervous systems become depleted and exhausted. We may have panic attacks and be in a constant state of trepidation and dread. When fear is at its most intense, we may experience terror. Our nervous systems are naturally relaxed when we feel safe. When we become fearful, everything inside us runs amok with nervous energy, restlessness and hyper vigilance. We are unable to settle on anything, constantly on the move and unable to relax. We don't really focus on anything, as we get constantly distracted and disturbed by the strain of having to keep a watch out for dangers and threats. Our bodies remain stiff and unrelaxed — we literally hold ourselves tensely and stiffly, consciously or unconsciously. This certainly takes a physical toll on our bodies.

In climate discussions some people think fear can be a motivator to stir humanity into action. I believe that people respond better to risks when given both a reason and a way to act.

I am fascinated by how the article by David Wallace-Wells "When Will Climate Change Make the Earth Too Hot For Humans?"[28] published in *New York Magazine* went viral and became the most-read story in the magazine's history. It presents a worst-case climate peril scenario which I found very frightening to read. The article begins with the words "It is, I promise, worse than you think. If your anxiety about global warming is dominated by fears of sea-level rise, you are barely scratching the surface of what terrors are possible, even within the lifetime of a teenager today." This is the opposite of selling the dream, it is predicting the hell. Which approach motivates you to act, the hopeful dream or the fearful hell? The presence antidote to fear is love.

Stuckness

Everything is energy, including our bodies. This energy is constantly moving and flowing unless we feel stuck. Stagnation in our energy causes us to lose touch with our natural flow. We tire easily and may feel drained and lacklustre. In stuckness we feel unable to act or to turn in a specific direction, as we become emotionally and physically static. Paralysing thoughts and emotions may swirl around our nervous systems, minds and hearts. We get caught in the freeze response. Everything feels slow, stagnant and impossible. We may become more and more static and turn inwards.

Constantly associating climate peril with doom, gloom, and disaster can inhibit any action on our part. Faced with an overwhelming threat, we can feel less motivated to act. Espen Stoknes, in *What We Think About When We Try Not to Think About Global Warming* (2015), explores how the more some people learn about climate change, the less they act to limit it: a process he calls the "snooze button effect." He offers five solutions to stay engaged and act; make the climate peril narrative social, make being low-carbon simple, focus on opportunities, sell the dream not the hell and use climate-relevant signals that people can connect to. The presence antidote to stuckness is flow.

Anxiety Immobilised Impact

One of the two Anxiety Impacts is being Immobilised. This is the place where we completely lose all of our agency and feel unable to act. For some people, having to face incredibly difficult truths about our climate future may cause them to feel that it is pointless doing anything at all. Another way of being immobilised is to feel that you are not important enough or that only doing large or very public actions matter.

Have you ever felt your stomach churning or your heart racing while you worry about the imminent end of the world as we know it? Or maybe you get a feeling of existential dread creep up on you whenever you hear news about some aspect of climate peril. If you feel it is already too late and that we are doomed, what happens to you?

We are immobilised when the freeze response kicks in and we are literally unable to move, to act or to feel active in any way. The freeze response happens when our brains are unable to respond to a threat or feel unable to move away from the threat. We literally freeze by remaining still, unable to move, totally numb. We may dissociate from our bodies. Immobilisation and freezing are built-in defence mechanisms that cause physiological changes, including rapid heart rate and reduced perception of pain, enabling you to protect yourself by releasing endorphins which calm your body, helping to relieve the stress and anxiety. They are responses to a threatening or dangerous experience that is too difficult to process. Grounding and bringing ourselves into presence can alleviate the freeze response and get us moving again. If we can feel into our own natural born gifts and talents, we can inspire others to step up and out, to act and be embodied despite inclination not to. Acting can move us out of the lethargy and sense of despair that underpins being immobilised. The antidote to being Immobilised is Embodiment.

Anxiety Immobilised Results

There are three Anxiety Results stemming from being Immobilised. These are Burnout, Self-interest and Unhealthy Relationships.

Burnout

Burnout is one of the biggest challenges facing activists who work tirelessly for their cause and may be protesting for long periods of time where the living conditions are not comfortable. They may gradually feel that being an activist has become a heavy burden, rather than the embodiment of joy and right action. It is draining and demotivating when key influencers are not listening or acting and climate disasters grow day by day. A form of burnout is climate crisis fatigue: the helpless feeling that whatever you do is too little, too late. Tired activists can begin to ask, "what's the point?" when fossil fuels continue to be expanded and climate change promises are consistently broken. Burnout is a state of emotional, physical and mental exhaustion caused by excessive and prolonged stress. It occurs when we feel overwhelmed, emotionally drained and unable to meet constant demands. As the stress continues, we can begin to lose the interest or motivation that led us to take on an activist role in the first place. Common signs of burnout include feeling exhausted, difficulty concentrating and a sense of detachment or apathy. Instead of skilful, healthy relationships we create unhealthy relationships.

How we feel and how we look after our physical, mental and emotional well-being are crucial to prevent burnout, particularly when faced with the anxiety-inducing challenge of trying to save the world. I know this for myself, and I have heard lots of other activists say the same. There can be so few wins when you are fighting against a system that is built to resist challenge, change or new perspectives. If your sole aim in your activism is to win, you are likely to become cynical, frustrated and depleted.

My daughter Keri, and her husband Terry, were part of an anti HS2 campaign to stop a new high speed rail development in England. They protested for many years. At the point they realised they could not stop the development being financed by the UK government, they didn't stop protesting and continued for another ten years. They exhibited resilience, strength and trust in their own activism. They found ways of making their efforts more joyful, as well as disruptive. They were involved in dreary and pugnacious committees where they applied logical arguments to try to win benefits for the many people adversely affected by a lack of compensation. They also protested with a huge, inflatable, white elephant in various places including national political conferences and their local high street. They contributed to a winning judicial review at the UK Courts of Justice. They helped to create eye-catching, witty slogans, posters and stunts, as well as enjoyable gatherings and alliances. They never burned out because they valued every small win along the way. They understood the possibility of not preventing HS2 happening.

Extinction Rebellion has made numerous efforts to prevent burnout and build well-being into its movement. It has developed a fascinating, regenerative approach named "Regen" to emphasise self-care. The Extinction Rebellion protests I have attended in London provided nourishing food, well-being tents for self-care, massages, sharing groups and places to rest, as well as support to face internal feelings and concerns. When and individual is in presence, their Burnout is dissolved by Right Action.

Self-Interest

Instead of embodying the best of what we are possible in joyful and energetic service, we are caught in the grip of Self-interest. We don't do anything of value for others, and we only for ourselves in relation to climate peril or anything else. The opposite of selfless service is selfishness and being self-absorbed: everything we do, every response we make is only done through the lens of our own advantage. We feel unable to walk in someone else's shoes or unable to consider and value their perspective. The more anxious we are, the more we may lack the capacity to be interested in, or to have the bandwidth to give our energy to, anyone else. Many of the personality disorders of today have disconnection and self-interest at their core. Narcissism treats others as objects purely to meet the interests of the narcissist. I believe that we have the resources to end poverty and feed everyone. Yet self-interest means the wealthy keep their money and the poor get even poorer.

We have the resources to solve climate peril, yet the self-interest of key influencers preferring to keep profits from fossil fuel industries is destroying the planet. Wars are still being waged over geographical territory in a nation's own interest, regardless of the many people who get killed. For me, the worse part of self-interest is the lack of regard for, and the harm done to, others, as well as the disconnection that is painful for everyone involved. The self-interest and greed of fossil fuel companies is the main reason for preventing action on climate peril. When in presence Self-interest is dissolved by Service.

Unhealthy Relationships

Instead of co-cocreating and forming Healthy Relationships, we find ourselves in unhealthy ones. Unhealthy Relationships limit and damage everyone involved. They activate everyone's shadow, reactivity and childhood wounding. We may behave in ways that cause difficulties in our relationships, resulting in embarrassment and shame. Within relationships, our anxiety may lead to low self-esteem, self-criticism, blaming the other person, depression, shame, rage or jealousy. Irrational feelings and self-defeating behaviours can make us say things we regret and destroy harmony and openness. Toxic relationships get in the way of effective communication and being able to fulfil our maximum potential. We are unable to find what we want and need to keep growing and expanding.

We are living from our shadow personality when we find ourselves in relationships behaving in ways we don't want to behave, doing what we don't want to do, saying things we don't want to say and feeling as if we are out of control. This is because an energy or wounding, which was placed unconsciously into our childhood shadow bag from a particular experience, has remained within our unconscious. It gets activated in the current relationship situation because it mirrors the original situation from childhood. Any outburst or reactivity, often with a strong energetic charge, can feel draining and constricting. It de-energises and diminishes our responsiveness and our confidence. It can prevent us from being appropriate and skilful. Presence helps us to see the destructiveness and self-harm in our relationships and to find how we can be different and move into healthy relationships.

The essences arise to assist our choices and behaviours. When we are in presence, our Unhealthy Relationships are dissolved into Healthy Relationships.

Anxiety Denial Impact

The second Anxiety Impact is Denial. Denial can stop us from feeling anxious through being out of touch with what is really happening in the world. In some ways, it is a useful defence mechanism. Maintaining denial in the face of overwhelming evidence and information on climate peril can be exhausting. To take threats seriously, most people need to feel fully informed before they can offer a well-considered opinion. The abundance of contradictory information on climate peril can be overwhelming or confusing, making it very difficult to form your own, clear opinion. Overwhelm and confusion can lead to denial.

Denial has a survival function, as it is an important mechanism for helping us to protect ourselves from too much anxiety, fear and overwhelm. Our brains cope well with immediate threats, yet we are not wired to perceive the dangers of long-term, systemic threats. We are the boiling frogs who are being informed and affected so gradually by climate information, issues and impacts that we constantly absorb, rationalise, habituate and minimise what is happening. The result is a denial that enables us to carry on with our lives and to function. It can be too difficult to face the possibility of our lives being severely disrupted and changed for the worse, so we reject this as a possibility. Most people are averse to change and hang onto the status quo or find ways of denying and avoiding what makes them feel uncomfortable.

There are a range of organisations and think tanks engaged in campaigns to encourage climate denial. They actively disseminate information serving their own self-interest, and deliberately deny or distort the scientific data on climate peril. The data, science and modeling of climate impact is very complex, contradictory, controversial and variable, making denial a less anxiety-inducing option than choosing to see a potentially disastrous future.

Mark Maslin, in *How to Save Our Planet: The Facts* (2021), illustrates deliberate attempts from scientific, political, economic and humanitarian perspectives to deny that we are in a deep crisis and need to act. His focus on the many forms of denial is illuminating. He emphasises how denial is a "very human emotion" and "facts are power."

Clive Hamilton, in *Requiem for a Species: Why We Resist the Truth About Climate Change* (2010), feels that continuing in denial eventually "becomes perverse," requiring one of following denial approaches: "a wilful misreading of the science, a romantic view of the ability of political institutions to respond or faith in divine intervention."

I have always been fascinated by how we live each day with death all around us and yet we are able to carry on and live our daily lives. There is a Hindu saying that we wake up every day thinking we are immortal when all around us is death. We all accept, on some level, however unconscious, that we will die, that death is an inevitability, yet it's only when death is imminent that we fully face our own individual immortality.

To come out of denial we need support to face the psychological, emotional and physical impacts that can arise. In my approach, the antidote to denial is having illuminations that shift us from feelings of separation and isolation into the perception and truth of interdependence, different views of realities and different senses of self. When in presence, Denial is dissolved by Illumination.

Anxiety Denial Results

We live in Denial through the three Anxiety Results of Shadow Personality, Inner Critic and Separation.

Shadow Personality

The word shadow is a mythological name invented by Carl Jung. A useful metaphor is "our shadow bag," a term created by Robert Bly in *A Little Book on the Human Shadow* (1988). Our shadow bag fills up in the first half of life, as a depository for all those characteristics of personality that are disowned. We may spend up to twenty years putting content into our shadow bag and the rest of our life retrieving, revealing and healing the contents to restore our wholeness. We may be placing aspects of our relationship with climate peril into our shadow bag. I wonder what the shadow bags of Generation Z are filled with.

Our unconscious bias, constrictions and reactive personality qualities are called the shadow because you cannot see them. They sit beyond sight, in unknown or unseen parts of ourselves. Shadow is usually associated with negative aspects, yet we can also hold our finest qualities in our shadow. By refusing or being unable to own either, we project them on to others. Our shadow includes the things about ourselves that we deny and the things our caretakers, culture, peers or communities didn't want, approve of or accept: anything subdued, criticised or deemed unacceptable.

It helps to identify, to be present with, then to move through and dissolve our destructive behaviours, thoughts and actions. Shadow work is an important part of learning to be deeply present, skilful, authentic and responsive. Understanding and releasing our shadow can help us access presence more easily, as there are less blockages in the way of essence arising. It also increases our energy and frees us, mentally, emotionally and physically. We experience greater inner freedom to pause, to be in presence and to make conscious choices, accepting both the light and dark in ourselves.

When we can access different senses of self, as explored in Chapter 8, and realise that we are not only our constructed personality, then we can see, heal and move beyond our Shadow

Personality. Our Shadow Personality is dissolved by expanded Senses of Self.

Separation

Separation means the moving away of something, being apart from something or someone, not being together, being divided, being pulled apart or not united. In separation there is a gap between two or more people or things. Everything in our society leads us to believe that we are separate entities; we live inside our bodies and minds while others live in their bodies and minds which are different and separate. I am me; you are other. We learn to think and speak in a subject and object paradigm, and that becomes our reality. We see the world through discrete, separate objects. This leads to constant comparisons, competition and judgement. Separation is a useful way of navigating the conventional world, but it is not the only reality as explored in Chapter 8.

Part of the mythology of separation is the perspective of nature-as-thing, generating the belief that only human beings are possessed of full selfhood. This is what licenses us to exploit nature for our own ends, and to see everyone and everything else as "other." If we drop out of the interconnection view of reality, we cannot see beyond opposites and separateness. We lose all sense of deeper realities that can help us to cope with climate anxiety and solve its negative impacts. We may feel alienated, isolated and unable to connect to people, animals, nature and the planet as a living breathing entity that gives us life. The potential ending of the world, the climate peril, feels like an utterly horrible catastrophe that is the end of everyone and everything.

Steve Taylor's latest book, *Disconnected: The Roots of Human Cruelty and How Connection Can Heal the World* (2023), views connection as the most essential human trait for goodness, right action and well-being. He explores how cruelty and pathocracy are a result of disconnection and separation, leading to toxic, dominator, oppressive, patriarchal, hierarchical and warlike societies. He argues that connected societies are more egalitarian, democratic and peaceful. I agree with him that regaining awareness of our connection (or interconnection) is the only way in which we can live in harmony with ourselves, one another, the world and our planet. Interconnection, beyond all sense of separation, is a key perspective of Presence Activism. In presence, Separation is dissolved by Interconnection.

Inner Critic

The Inner Critic is an internal voice that berates or criticises us for doing whatever action we are doing, or for having any experience we are having. All of us have an inner critic voice. It is constantly attacking, judging and making us feel wrong, bad or deficit. It can heighten anxiety, depress energy and make us feel negative, guilty, ashamed, hopeless, devalued, small and vulnerable. Significant obstacles to presence include all the beliefs, structures, judgements and childhood conditioning whirling around inside our heads, criticising us and holding us back.

Once, our inner critics were useful to us, especially in our early childhood because they helped us to identify, clarify and organise our experiences. As we get older, we find that anything within our inner critic that no longer serves us can be restricting, debilitating and blocking, causing significant suffering. It gets in the way of accessing presence and pursuing a deeper inquiry into our different senses of self (explored in Chapter 8).

Fighting or going against my inner critic has not worked for me. Rather than going rigid and defending against my inner critic, presence has dissolved it in a way that is gentle, loving and enhancing. Living in presence has enabled me to gain a deeper sense of compassion towards myself and to stop saying and thinking harsh words. I have become kinder to myself and others.

Accessing different and expanded views of reality has prevented me from becoming stuck inside the negative, repeating voice and patterns of my inner critic. They have let me see that the worst aspects of my personality are not fixed. In presence, my inner critic disappears.

When in presence, our Inner Critic is dissolved by different Views of Reality, explored in Chapter 8.

***

In addition to all the things we have to face externally regarding climate peril, we also need to face these anxious inner states and blocked energies. Moving deeply into, and through, all these anxiety states and experiences will liberate us into skilful activism. The Presence Flower and profound experiences of presence enable and support us to move through all the petals of climate anxiety. We need to face the depths of our anxiety, to journey again and again from anxiety into presence to allow the presence essences to dissolve our anxiety. When we can allow the most appropriate essence(s) to arise in any situation, we can make conscious choices and respond in skilful ways as Presence Activists

In the next chapter I explore Presence Activism in relation to other climate activists and climate movements.

Chapter 5

Presence Activism and Climate Activism

***

"And let us not pray to be sheltered from dangers, but to be fearless when facing them." **Rabindranath Tagore**

***

Introduction

I have created Presence Activism as a path of radical disruption through understanding, experiencing and practicing presence in the midst of action. I have developed Presence Activism from my own journey as an activist, as well as from learning about other activists alongside whom I have journeyed. This chapter describes Presence Activism and explores relevant climate activists and movements, especially those by which I have been influenced.

I want Presence Activism to equip a wide range of people to cope with the myriad challenges and anxieties of these turbulent times and to help anyone wanting to be simultaneously active and grounded, living beyond any anxiety. Of course, Presence Activism needs to be accompanied by huge systemic changes in solving climate peril such as those proposed by the scientists, activists, think tanks, policy agencies, climate summits, commentators and writers on climate peril I have included in this book.

Presence Activism is intended for anyone new to the practice and concept of presence, as well as those already ensconced in and familiar with presence. It is an invitation to live and act from kinship, interconnection and deep awareness of the preciousness of life. It stems from a direct and visceral knowing of presence in all its shapes and influences.

As an activist in the UK, I want to acknowledge the privileges I have in being able to protest freely despite the more punitive sentences being made in the UK courts. In many countries climate protest can be met with imprisonment and even the death penalty.

Presence Activism

At the core of Presence Activism is the discernment of how a deeper wisdom is asking us to show up, engage and act. Presence Activism is effortless and flows in alignment with our unique purpose for the repair and restoration of Mother Earth. We act consistently for the higher good, well-being and maximum potential of everyone and all beings.

Accessing the seven Presence Essences releases the stamina to stay involved in challenging climate peril for the long haul. Practising the Presence and Anxiety Flowers will help us to stay present enough to face the worst perils of climate emergency, while simultaneously acting to make a difference. Allowing the seven Presence Essences to dissolve climate anxiety becomes a constant support in navigating our way through whatever faces us on a daily basis, enabling us to become skilled in being both active and present, with our own unique flavour.

Presence Activism enables each one of us to be the most expanded we can be, understanding that our states of being, our senses of self and our views of reality matter as much as our actions. We don't burn out or become overly anxious when our actions flow from a sense of being grounded, boundless, whole, interconnected and abundant. Presence Activism constantly brings us back to each other, to the Earth in service, to right action and to healthy relationships. When we do our inner work of deep transformation, our activism becomes an opportunity to grow, develop and offer sacred service rather than be in an exhausting, angry reactive fight against an enemy. We change the world by knowing, understanding and changing ourselves.

We understand that what we do to another, we do to ourselves, as we are not separate from each other, from all beings or from the earth. Every person we encounter, and every experience we have becomes a mirror to reflect something that is in ourselves. We are an integral part of a universal web and flow of life, working towards optimisation amidst the threat of societal collapse and an endangered planet.

Presence Activism is organically nonviolent. Erica Chenoweth and Maria J. Stephan, in *Why Civil Resistance Works: The Strategic Logic of Nonviolent Conflict* (2011), evidence that between 1900 and 2006 campaigns of nonviolent resistance were more than twice as effective as their violent counterparts. The key to success is the 3.5% rule which posits that no government can stand up to that share of the population mobilising against it. Extinction Rebellion have taken achievement of this figure as a core part of their strategy. Successful movements use varied approaches including lobbying, campaigning, protesting, striking and civil disobedience.

Climate Activism

New forms of activist protest movements are gaining traction and grassroots initiatives are making a difference. Powerful multiracial, global and intergenerational coalitions are using eco-positive, antiracist and feminist principles to mobilise transformative change to bring attention to the climate crisis and to stop further destruction. As a lifelong feminist, I have witnessed and lived through second, third and fourth wave feminisms, including eco-feminism. I am delighted to see a resurgence of feminism in the 2020s.

Young and old activists, communities most at risk and those with the fewest resources, as well as progressive politicians and some public sector leaders, are generating radical demands and are calling for radical change. I recommend exploring two interesting activist women, both cofounders of high-profile protest movements: Gail Bradbrook of Extinction Rebellion and Alicia Garza of Black Lives Matter. Alicia Garza's book, *The Purpose of Power* (2020), is a compelling description of co-creating a successful activist mass movement. She describes leading the movement through being leaderful rather than leaderless. Her book is a significant contribution to new forms of successful global activism. Gail Bradbrook is active on YouTube and online.

For many, peaceful activism is the foundation of protest. Others draw on violent means. One of the activist paths I really admire is that of non-violent resistance. Three heroes of mine who pioneered nonviolent ways of co-creating and inspiring mass movements are Gandhi, Martin Luther King and Nelson Mandela in his post-prison years. They brought about extraordinary results without acting violently; however, much violence was done against them.

The numerous activist climate movements that exist today continue to offer disruptive actions through every means possible. There are millions of individuals and thousands of groups, from all walks of life, holding climate protests all over the world, including disruptions, protests, marches, demands, sit-downs, die-ins, peoples' assemblies and pickets.

The most inspiring activists today are not only saying that we should no longer put carbon into the atmosphere; they are also saying that we should build a better world in which compassionate and regenerative solutions, rather than selfish and destructive ones, are central.

Many people who protest on the streets continue to act and challenge despite all the odds. They share and shout their truth, and they energetically build creative and sophisticated alliances and networks. They work towards building positive new ways forward rather than simply condemning and attempting to destroy the dreadful things all around them.

The Extinction Rebellion and Just Stop Oil campaigns have brought climate peril into public consciousness. They have also experienced mighty forces of reaction against them in many different countries. In the UK new punitive laws are being proposed to control demonstrations and to bring about a fierce curtailing of human rights and civil disobedience.

Generation Z

Generation Z, also known as iGen, Gen Z or Zoomers, was born in the mid to late 1990s to the early 2010s. In 2023, they are aged around thirteen to twenty-eight. They succeed Millennials and precede Generation Alpha. Another name for this age group is the "climate generation," as they are the first generation to have spent their whole life living with the effects of climate peril and are the generation most prone to climate anxiety. They care deeply about global warming and have to live daily with the inherited results of previous generations who are destroying the planet to reap the benefits of an extractive, fossil fuel-based lifestyle. This generation has inherited the Anthropocene Age, a geological age in which humans have irreversibly, and adversely, affected the climate and environment. My two granddaughters are both Gen Z. My eldest granddaughter and Greta Thunberg are the same age, twenty in 2023.

I am aware of my privilege and limited perspective as a white woman living in the West within a rural community. There are thousands of Generation Z climate activists making a huge difference within their own countries. I honour them all. Two websites name and celebrate some of them: Flores Gaby's article, "Meet 12 climate activists changing the world" (2021),[29] and Tess Lowery's article, "20 Climate Activists & Organizations to Watch at COP27" (2022).[30] I include the names of the young climate activists they mention out of respect and admiration: Marinel Ubaldo, Philippines; Vanessa Nakate, Uganda; Ineza Umuhoza Grace, Rwanda; Txai Suruí, Brazil; Leala Pourier,

Pine Ridge Indian Reservation; Aisha Akbar, Pakistan; Maytik Avirama, Colombia; Yared Abera, Ethiopia; Samara Assunção, Brazil; Hindou Oumarou Ibrahim, Chad; India Logan-Riley (Ngāti Kahungunu, Rongomaiwahine, Rangitāne), Aotearoa; Ryan Bestre, Philippines; Nyombi Morris, Uganda; Elizabeth Wathuti, Kenya; Ayisha Siddiqua, Pakistan; Nathalia Lawen, Seychelles; Jayathma Wickramanayake, Sri Lanka; Evans Muswahili, Kenya; Jane Meriwas, Kenya; Mitzi Jonelle Tan, Philippines; Brianna Fruean, Samoa; Sophia Kianni, Iranian American.

Britt Way wrote *Generation Dread: Finding Purpose in an Age of Climate Crisis* (2022) at the age of thirty-three. She shares the wide range of climate issues facing young people today, including her personal dilemma of "reproductive anxiety" of choosing whether to have children or not. She asks the pertinent question, "Can she or he thrive in the calamitous future coming at us?" I love how when she did decide to get pregnant her "advocacy for climate justice became even fiercer." She concludes her book with the insight that the best way forward is "feeling the pain, anger, and heartbreak, and choosing to invest in the future anyway."

Inspired by Swedish student Greta Thunberg, 1.4 million young people from Generation Z, from all over the world, chose to engage in climate school strikes in 2019. The school strikes are a wonderful example of young people stepping up. Greta Thunberg, and her powerful protest, offers us a glimpse into how young people are feeling. The book she edited, *The Climate Book* (2022), is an invaluable and informative compendium of well-known climate writers, scientists and activists sharing their views on the urgency of climate change. On a recent visit to Stockholm, I accidentally met Greta and have nothing but admiration for her passion, humour, determination and open challenges to key influencers. She had a beautiful presence and was warm and approachable. She inspires all generations and is a valuable role model for how anyone can make an impact if they care enough. I believe her popularity expresses a climate peril zeitgeist for many young people. Her words went viral when she made these provocative statements at the United Nations Climate Change Conference, COP24, in 2018. "Since our leaders are behaving like children, we will have to take the responsibility they should have taken long ago," and "Why should I be studying for a future that soon may be no more, when no one is doing anything to save that future?" My favourite quote of hers from the Davos World Economic Forum in 2019 is, "I want you to act as if the house is on fire, because it is."

In May 2023 students across Europe occupied twenty-two schools and universities to protest inaction on the climate emergency. These occupations were part of a mass movement campaign, which continued on from the 2019 youth climate strike movement, led by "End Fossil: Occupy!"[31] Through disrupting, blockading, interrupting and sabotaging, these courageous students wanted to inspire all of society to take radical action with them. Their goals are to end the fossil fuel-based economy at an international level and to radicalise the youth climate movement.

Students Organising for Sustainability[32] is another young people's movement. It is good to see schoolteachers also acting through SDGTeachin.[33]

Mikaela Loach is a Jamaican-British climate activist who was named by Forbes as one of the most influential women in the UK climate movement. She has written *It's Not That Radical: Climate Action to Transform Our World* (2023). I encourage you to read her book. She provides a radical perspective on how to act on climate change. Her purpose is to mobilise people to campaign against climate peril. She especially advocates challenging new fossil fuel projects. She wants a "climate-just world for all" that goes beyond white environmentalism. This involves leaving behind the harmful system of whiteness, dismantling Euro-centric understandings of the climate crisis, and putting an end to the false truths of white supremacy, colonialism and capitalism. She advocates transformative visions, eco and Indigenous-led socialism and a future of coalitions focussed on both lifestyle changes and systemic change. She urges rich nations, which have historically caused the climate crisis, to transition their economies and to transfer wealth to the Global South countries.

She advocates the greenwashing and greentrolling of self-interested corporates who care only about profits and have no intention of changing. She has no trust in them and proposes removing any "social licence" by disrupting and making their climate destroying activities impossible. She calls for a "Just Transition" away from harmful fossil fuels to renewable energy.

Extinction Rebellion

Extinction Rebellion is a movement of activists who are trying to prevent the extinction of humans and all species caused by climate change and social collapse. Building upon, and learning from, activist history, Extinction Rebellion went viral in 2017 with their civil disobedience protests. They brought attention and action to the climate crisis through non-violent means. They have had a huge impact on bringing the climate emergency into public consciousness.

Their cofounders had studied previous activist movements and tried to do things effectively based on their studies and understanding. It began in the UK and quickly spread, becoming a distributed network with bases in sixty other cities. I am an Extinction Rebellion rebel and have taken part in three large, organised street protests in London. Its first large-scale protest was in London in April 2019. I was there. It was an extraordinary event, full of life and commitment and anticipation. It was hugely successful in bringing all the issues of climate peril into the public discourse, attracting Extinction Rebellion rebels from many different age groups and backgrounds. It engaged in attention-grabbing, disruptive protests and focused on getting as many people arrested as possible.

Gradually public opinion changed as parts of Extinction Rebellion undertook more radical, disruptive acts that were unnecessarily affecting people going about their work. In October 2019 they held another large-scale protest with 800 arrests in three days. They made three demands: that the government does more to communicate the urgency of the climate crisis; that it legally commits to net-zero carbon emissions by 2025; and that a citizens' assembly be convened to oversee the changes. Another two-week series of protests began on August 23, 2021, under the name "Impossible Rebellion," followed in 2022 by an April Rebellion and then the September Rebellion. In early 2023 they made a statement saying, "we quit," and stopped focusing on severe disruption and getting arrested as their main tactics. They turned their attention and energy to growing a broader mass movement, less extreme tactics and a wide network of climate partners.

In April 2023 there was a major non-violent protest called The Big One. It took place over four days in London and attracted over 60,000 people. Speakers called out the right-wing press, corporates, self-interested lobbyists, the banks and other bastions of power fundamental to creating and continuing the climate crisis. Along with many thousands of others, including family and friends, I went on this Extinction Rebellion national protest. It was an incredible experience, stimulating and exciting. There was also a massive frustration at the lack of progress by governments and corporates. I am still bemused and disappointed that millions did not turn up. I was horrified to hear more stories of the UK government considering giving licenses to oil companies to exploit new oil fields. This is also happening elsewhere in the world despite the March 2023 Intergovernmental Panel on Climate Change (IPCC) stating there must be no new fossil fuel development if the world is to limit global heating to 1.5 degrees Celsius.

The Red Rebel Brigade[34] is manifesting climate activism through silent presence. I find the members extraordinarily powerful as they walk slowly and dramatically, in silence, through Extinction Rebellion protests. They move in a synchronous unity. They dress stylishly in red flowing robes, their faces painted white with sad expressions. They dress in red to generate both aesthetic and symbolic emotive responses and to symbolise the common blood shared by all species. My favourite lines from their website are, "We illuminate the magic realm beneath the surface of all things, and we invite people to enter in, we make a bubble and calm the storm, we are peace in the midst of war. We are who the people have forgotten to be!"

Civil and Uncivil Disobedience

Due to the lack of response by governments and corporates on taking effective action on climate peril, debates are taking place today amongst activists regarding whether nonviolent protest is having enough effect and if it is now time to engage in more violent protest, particularly against property.

Many activist movements, including the Suffrage movement, that began non-violently eventually turned to attacks on property when they felt unheard. Extinction Rebellion has split into differing factions over the use of drones at Heathrow airport, and Gail Bradbrook deliberately broke a window to get arrested. Like the suffragettes and other activist movements, modern climate activists are considering what to do next to have more impact when governments and other key influencers do not take speedy action. The continuation and expansion of fossil use, the resistance to funding resilient ecosystems, the refusal to heed scientific warnings and reluctance to tackle the climate peril over many years is immensely frustrating for climate activists, especially generation Z.

I think we are at a potential turning point as to whether peaceful protesting will soon turn into acts of violence in the face of such extreme global climate inaction.

Andreas Malm, in his Guardian article "The moral case for destroying fossil fuel infrastructure" (2021)[35] and his book *How to Blow Up a Pipeline* (2021), draws upon the history of social justice movements to argue that property destruction should be considered as a valid tactic in the pursuit of environmental justice. He advocates for the climate movement to escalate its responses in order to force fossil fuel extraction to stop, to defuse and destroy "its tools" and to start blowing up oil pipelines. Malm argues that the strategic acceptance of property destruction and violence has been the only route for revolutionary change. He describes how historically frustrated activists have turned from peaceful campaigning into militancy and violent protest, despite the ethics of pacifism and nonviolence. He describes how violence became an element of many activist protests when their demands were ignored. Examples include fighting slavery, stopping the further colonisation of India, ending apartheid, fighting for women's right to vote and the Arab spring uprising. He argues that violence will become inevitable, and necessary, for activists to succeed in bringing about effective change on climate issues. He suggests a "radical flank" of activists willing to demolish, burn, blow up, and use any means necessary.

The film version of the book, released in 2023, directed by Daniel Goldhaber, features a fictional group of eight young people in West Texas who blow up an oil pipeline in two key locations. I found it a compelling watch that explores both the inner and outer tensions of making the kind of violent choices these youngsters ultimately make, each for very different reasons. I have huge sympathy with their frustrations, intentions and sentiments, yet I personally will always choose non-violence. To choose civil or violent disobedience and protest will always be an ongoing moral dilemma while serious injustice and oppression exists. I believe we each have to make our own personal choice.

Many groups are undertaking more radical disruption all over the world. Protesters from Declare Emergency and Just Stop Oil, as well as climate activists in all parts of the world, have targeted galleries and museums to deface or glue themselves to works of arts. They have also disrupted several high profile national events. They do so because they believe that key influencers are not listening, and time is running out. They are receiving strong sentences in the courts, as some governments are making activists into terrorists, introducing draconian prison sentences and increasing fines. Just Stop Oil protests demand no new oil and gas extraction in the North Sea and they act to stop the gears of production through "ecotage" with the aim of protecting the environment.

While Malm advocates violence, George Monbiot in his Guardian article "I back saboteurs who have acted with courage and coherence, but I won't blow up a pipeline. Here's why" (2023)[36] does not agree with using violence, even though it may be morally justifiable. He feels climate challenges are so complex and intertwined that violence will ultimately not work, as it will generate violent responses in return. He advocates that "our best hope is to precipitate a social tipping: widening the concentric circles of those committed to systemic change until a critical threshold is reached, that flips the status quo."

I can see value and downsides in both their arguments, and I encourage you to decide upon your own violent or nonviolent activist path. For me, Presence Activism is nonviolent.

Sacred Activism

My Presence Activism approach, while innovative with its integral focus on presence and action, also has commonality with other activists and writers' approaches, including those of Gail Bradbrook, Andrew Harvey, Joanna Macy, Satish Kumar, James O'Dea, John Robinson and Starhawk.

Several activists have found the transpersonal or sacred aspects of dealing with climate peril and climate anxiety to be vital for them as a strong source of support and nourishment. This is also true for me. Many Pagans draw upon earth-based rituals and sacred approaches in their climate activism. Others rely upon a more esoteric or conventional spiritual underpinning. The sacred has often played an important role for activists who work through non-violence or Ahimsa: a Jain, Buddhist and Hindu doctrine expressing belief in the sacredness of all living creatures and urging the avoidance of harm and violence.

The powerful book edited by Wahinke Topa (Four Arrows) and Darcia Narvaez, *Restoring the Kinship World View: Indigenous Voices Introduce 28 Precepts for Rebalancing Life on Planet Earth* (2022), provides 28 Indigenous precepts from original Indigenous understanding and ancestral wisdom. It contains the most beautiful and gracious array of Kinship worldviews, articulating the nature-based consciousness so needed in the world today. Another significant book of Indigenous wisdom specifically designed to be a support to anyone seeking ideas and responses to climate issues is *We Are the Middle of Forever: Indigenous Voices from Turtle Island on the Changing Earth,* edited by Dahr Jamil and Stan Rushworth (2022).

Indigenous societies have a much more integrated relationship to earth and its "member beings." A Kincentric worldview is very different from Eurocentric mindsets which are steeped in domination, extraction, colonisation and separation from nature—a mindset that has depleted our planet for far too long. These two books made a powerful impression upon me, especially the descriptions of how colonialists have treated Indigenous tribes appallingly and destroyed their lands and ways of life. The insights, through different voices, into how Indigenous communities experienced loss and suffering are vital to respect and recall. Learning from their experience can help the world stop the same brutality and mistakes from ever being made again.

Indigenous people manage land and other resources completely differently from the dominating and ravaging methods employed in colonialism. The Kinship perspective of managing land resources harmoniously and effectively for future generations is one desperately needed across the whole world. Pre-colonised Indigenous cultures have consistently nurtured lifestyles that respect, cultivate and regenerate the diversity, complexity, integrity and health of nature, of the biosphere and of all living beings. They are also the people most harmed and threatened by brutal, exploitative colonial practices and violence. Many Indigenous peoples have been voicing warnings and despair, as their identities and ways of life are ravaged and destroyed by human-created climate and ecological changes. European colonisation is inextricably connected to the dispossession of Indigenous peoples' land, and to the global expansion of fossil fuel use.

Andrew Harvey, in *The Hope: A Guide to Sacred Activism* (2009), writes about the importance of "compassion-in-action" born of a fusion of deep spiritual knowledge, courage, love, and passion with wise radical action. He set up the Institute of Sacred Activism as an essential force for preserving and healing the planet and its inhabitants.[37] He proposes a new movement of activists who act while surrendering the fruits of their action to the Divine. His activism comprises compassionate service married to a practical and pragmatic drive to transform all existing economic, social and political institutions. His approach calls for radical, "holy force" and "networks of grace" organised around professions, passions or whatever breaks our hearts. He advocates small cells of "Sacred Activists" who meet regularly and harness the energies of love, compassion and justice.

Harvey suggests five inner saboteurs that every Sacred Activist must face: disbelief, denial, dread, disillusion and the desire to cease existing. These are similar to my anxiety energies. Satish Kumar is an impressive environmental and peace activist, founder of the Schumacher College in Devon and editor of the magazine *Resurgence & Ecologist*. He speaks on nature, climate, environmental issues and activism in his various books and articles. I particularly like his book *Soil, Soul, Society: A New Trinity for Our Time* (2013). In an interesting interview titled *Talking the Walk,*[38] Kumar expresses his view that the spiritual aspect has been lost within the broader environmental movement because it has not understood the power of concepts such as love and reverence. He challenges the current, overly logical, analytical approach of climate activists. He also highlights their preference to focus on doom, gloom and disaster and says that the actions of environmentalists will lead to tears if they don't come from the place of the spirit. For him, "A battleground is an aberration," and he encourages Ahimsa. Kumar is a Jain, one of the most eco-conscious, ancient faith traditions. Jainism holds nature in deep respect and reverence.

I admire Professor Atul K. Shah and his pioneering activism of sharing what can be learnt from the ancient faith of Jainism and its ecological focus. He works tirelessly to expose the ways in which banks and asset managers continue to invest in the fossil fuel industries that are destroying nature, communities and society. He is making a significant challenge to the global finance industry and the greed underpinning it in his book co-authored with Aidan Rankin, *Jainism and Ethical Finance* (2017).

I often turn to Jain scriptures and writings, as they hold ancient and profound ecological wisdom that is seriously needed in the world today.

The pioneer of eco-activism Starhawk bridges the worlds of activism, Wicca, Goddess spirituality and Earth spirituality. She sees any perceived dichotomy between spirituality and politics as a middle-class, Western notion because in many cultures, particularly Indigenous and Eastern ones, magic, spirituality, activism and politics are not separate. In the 1970s, Starhawk restored women's activism, creating sacred places and ritual practices to re-enchant the world. Starhawk's work has continuously advocated for an engaged, political-activist, Goddess spirituality and for a revival of earth-based spirituality through her worldwide Reclaiming Movement.[39] I recommend her work, especially *The Spiral Dance: A Rebirth of the Ancient Religion of the Great Goddess* (1979) and *The Earth Path: Grounding Your Spirit in the Rhythms of Nature* (2006).

Gail Bradbrook, a co-founder of Extinction Rebellion, is a Pagan and sees her activism through an integration of the sacred, ecological, social, political and economic. Extinction Rebellion contains many rebels who openly express their spirituality and feel that it keeps them resilient and non-violent.

John Robinson, in *Mystical Activism: Transforming a World in Crisis* (2020), draws on presence as a way into mystical consciousness. His "mystical activism of self-transformation" is a here and now activism. He focuses on transforming ourselves, not by convincing others or by forcing institutions to change, but by co-creating an individual and collective experience of consciousness and reality. This shift in consciousness allows life to happen spontaneously, from divine consciousness. He encourages activists to wake up and to become "God, in motion" within an unpremeditated, unpredictable, unprescribed and unselfconscious activism.

James O'Dea, in *The Conscious Activist: Where Activism Meets Mysticism* (2015), combines spiritual knowledge with radical action in his handbook of sacred activism. Like me, he is a mystic and advocates a balanced fusion between inner spiritual growth and outer social activism to spark an accelerated transition towards a more evolved society. He makes a call for conscious activists to go beyond conformity and conventional structures of power and control.

Jem Bendell includes conceptions of the sacred through his R of Reverence. Originally, he offered his 4 Rs of Resilience, Relinquishment, Restoration and Reconciliation, later adding the fifth R of Reverence. He now gives attention and credence to wisdom traditions, including Indigenous wisdoms, as well as Eastern and Western mystical traditions. He is receiving guidance on spirituality from one of my dear friends Rev. Stephen Wright, an awesome, modern mystic whose book *Heartfullness: The Way of Contemplation: 12 Steps to Freedom, Awakening and the Beloved* (2021) is a delight of mystical wisdom and treasures. I can think of no one better than Stephen to advise Jem Bendell on his journey, as Stephen is profoundly connected into the importance of reverence, presence, mysticism and being in the now. If academics such as Jen Bendell can find comfort and value in the capacity of being more present and living in the moment so can many others, especially activists.

***

Presence Activism lies within the sacred activist paradigm and is also more expansive than this paradigm, as I have consciously used the words presence and transpersonal rather than spiritual and sacred throughout this book to be inclusive because some activists have issues with organised religion, or the word "spirituality." We can be present from exactly where we are and whatever our belief system.

I offer these different forms of activism to support you in ascertaining the underpinning of your own activism and to assist you in having a clear perspective on where Presence Activism sits within the broad world of activism. All of these activists and activist movements offer invaluable climate crisis actions and protests into the world. We each must follow our own path. Presence Activism is my chosen climate activist path offered as another approach. I explore how to embody Presence Activism in the next chapter.

Chapter 6

Embodying Presence Activism
in the World

***

"Let your presence ring out like a bell into the night."
Rainer Maria Rilke

***

Introduction

In the previous chapter I explored the nature of Presence Activism and how it relates to other climate movements. In this chapter I outline five stages of embodying presence, then share my path of living Presence Activism. I describe the Presence Flower Impact of Embodiment and the Presence Flower Embodiment Results of Service, Right Action and Healthy Relationships.

Embodying Presence Activism as an accessible and practical activist path can be far-reaching in its impact and contribution to climate peril. To that end I offer practical suggestions on how skilful activists embody presence by being fully in the world and fully of it through presence. Presence Activism is a profound, powerful change agent and transformer through which we can add value in the world, both through action and through the beingness of who we are at our highest potential and skilfulness.

Stages of Embodying Presence

While presence is always available, the nature of our relationship with presence constantly develops and shifts. I have discerned five stages of embodying presence in the world.

*Stage One: Being unconscious of presence
within the conventional world.*
For years we may be unaware of presence and live our lives, for better and worse, alternating between happiness and suffering, effectiveness and defeat. Our activism stems from constructed personality, reactivity and going against. We remain unconscious of our shadow self.

Stage Two: Being in the world with glimpses of presence.
We begin to consciously cultivate presence or have spontaneous experiences. We have glimpses and occasional experiences of presence and start to access one, several or all of the Presence Essences. Some of the essences remain elusive. We gain occasional relief from anxiety yet may still suffer. We learn how to experience presence more regularly within our daily lives. Presence is not yet our centre of gravity in our activism.

Stage Three: Being out of the world.
As we learn to access and experience presence more regularly, we may feel drawn to spending more and more time in presence. We need to be in solitude, or in conducive environments such as islands, forests, mountains, ashrams or monastic communities: places where there is sufficient peace, solitude or a holding structure that fosters us into being present. This is an important stage in which we shift from glimpses into a deeper and more consistent state of being in presence. This takes different amounts of time for different people. For those of us who cannot leave the world completely due to commitments, it is desirable to spend as much time as possible in retreat or in conducive places. In this stage we may be unable to be active in the world because our primary focus is on our inner world and alleviating our anxiety. Some people choose to live apart from the mainstream world for the rest of their lives.

Stage Four: Being in the world, yet not of it.
This stage is when we return from an isolated presence solitude or from distancing ourselves from the mainstream world. We continue to live our lives within the world, being in presence almost constantly. We are no longer ensconced within the perspectives of our constructed personality. We can see that the world is filled with people living from the limitations of their personality and shadow self. We remain non-attached and are able to access all the seven Presence Essences. Our anxieties are dissolved. This stage still has limitations, as it remains constructed from a belief that sees the material world as profane and lesser than the presence or spiritual domains. There remains a glimmer of separation of presence and profane.

Stage Five: Being in the world and fully of the world.
This view accepts both the material and physical world as fully permeated with presence. We are presence. There is no profane or any form of separation, even in suffering climate peril and difficulties. We experience presence in every aspect of the world. We are fully in the world and fully present within a continual dance of creative and dynamic intermingling. We abide directly and constantly in presence with liberation, equanimity and freedom from all overwhelm and anxiety. We are fully in the world, of the world and always fully present.

***

The world needs a critical mass of individuals and groups to work in stages four and five, through an integration of presence into their inner transformational path, simultaneously with living their outer path of activism in the world. My path is not to leave the world. For many years I wanted to be a nun and to live the contemplative path as in stage two. Eventually that stage passed, and I now enjoy being active within the world. I am most comfortable in the fifth stage, a path in which both my activism and inner work synthesise amidst whatever is arising.

Living My Presence Activism

I am grateful for the many years I have practised presence because it has given me a way, through being grounded sufficiently, to cope with the consequences and threats of climate peril, assisting me to stay calm and dissolve my anxiety. The seven Presence Essences have given me a practical and secure way of finding meaning, joy and calm in the midst of my activism.

Presence grounds, motivates and equips me to make a positive difference as a climate and feminist activist through a balance of stillness and action. Since 1989, presence has underpinned my activism and supported me in taking my actions to a whole new level without exhaustion or burnout.

I wasn't supported by presence in my first fifteen years of being an activist. I began my activism as an angry, second-wave feminist in 1974 when I went to university. I went on protests, stood on picket lines and undertook a wide range of disruptive acts, somehow managing to avoid arrest. With my sisters, we sometimes won but often lost many of the battles for gender equality. I frequently felt elated or exhausted. In the early 1980s, I was also active in the LGBT movement, the anti-nazi league, supporting the miners strikes, anti-nuclear movements and eco-feminism.

My early activism was steeped in fight rhetoric and a "going against" energy of anger and dissatisfaction. After my first profound presence experience in 1989, I needed to integrate my spirituality into my activism. I became an interfaith activist, bringing faith groups together to dialogue and collectively serve their communities. I consider all my thirty six years in Further Education to be offering service from a working-class, activist perspective, bringing about social justice primarily for working class students through vocational learning.

A significant presence shift happened for me in the mid 1990s. In hindsight, I can see how this was vital to my success and ability to keep going as a Presence Activist without burnout or derailment. I was feeling anxious, confused, disempowered and incompetent. I was alternating between constantly fighting against, being a warrior in battle against the establishment, and knowing that something "new" was needed from me yet not knowing what that something "new" was. I was feeling a need to move beyond my usual, belligerent comfort zone and that my current certainties, understanding and capabilities were not what were needed for the future. I was still focussed on doing, doing, doing and I became even more exhausted and confused. I found a mentor to create space to explore what was happening to me and to consider how I could do things differently while still being active. In the mentoring sessions, I began to see how fearful, protective and defensive I was. My emotional intelligence was low, my self-worth had hit rock bottom and I had feelings of anxiety, anger, guilt and blame about never changing anything. In one of the mentoring sessions, while sitting in silence and feeling confused beyond words, I had this presence experience.

***

"My awareness kept expanding, and I felt totally unified, within and without. The boundaries between myself and all that was around me dissolved, and my whole being expanded into spaciousness. I felt fully awake and present, completely here now, without any preconceptions or expectations, just the truth of what is here. Everything I knew about activism became a construct, an invention in my mind, as did everything I had ever known, all dissolving into a knowing that everything arises out of nothing, I have no self, there is only quietness, stillness, formlessness and emptiness at the core of everything, including me. I felt liberated, still and peaceful. I also felt full of possibilities. I felt a sense of pure unfolding, emerging out *of the stillness, bigger, better and more powerful than anything my conscious mind could imagine. All need for fighting vanished within the overwhelming sense of trust which transfused my whole body. I was unlimited and expansive with total acceptance of things as they are, being totally here now, non-attached to things. Everything, absolutely everything, was and would be well."*

***

This experience is constantly with me, in the midst of all my actions in the world. Since then, I can live my activism from an intrinsic response to others through interconnectedness and the seven Presence Essences. I opened to being active from the stillness and essences of presence, to balancing action and stillness. I also learnt how to use power with, for and_through_rather than over or against people. I now act in service from emergence, my activism flowing from spaciousness. This enables me to hold an open space for others to unfold, as well as for myself.

What I experience happening now in my activism is a continual emergence of new actions, possibilities, heathy relationships, service and right action out of being, presence and stillness.

Currently, I am a climate activist as an Extinction Rebellion rebel, attending their London protests for the past five years. I also work within my local community of Glastonbury, supporting individuals, community organisations and charities to develop their Luminary, leaderful, activist, autonomous and feminist leadership. I am a Priestess of Avalon supporting the rise of Goddess spirituality in the modern world as a radical, disruptive, feminist act. I am also acting locally to tackle climate issues in my community. I chair the Glastonbury Town Deal, a £23.6 million investment into my beloved town to support adapting and innovating locally within our community to make it as sustainable as it can be.

In my Luminary teachings and coaching I encourage activism through presencing. I have been told that it is my presence, pragmatic optimism, expertise and caring that supports people when they feel anxious. I know that all will be well and that we can achieve the impossible through a natural effulgence of service into the world through Presence Activism.

Presence Embodiment Impact and Results

To support you in embodying your own Presence Activism, I now describe the Presence Flower Impact of Embodiment and the Embodiment Results of Service, Right Action and Healthy Relationships. These are illustrated in figure 3 below to remind you of their place in the Presence Flower.

***

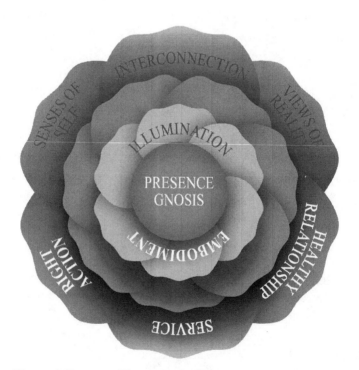

Figure 3 Presence Flower Embodiment Impact and Results

Presence Embodiment Impact

Presence Activism stems from a direct, visceral knowing of the seven Presence Essences: love, peace, flow, resilience, strength, trust and joy. Our activism feels different when we are acting with presence, ever accessible and abundant, always available to hold and support us in everything we are and do. Ideally, embodying Presence Activism feels natural and effortless, in alignment with our purpose on the planet. Profound embodiment of presence happens when the balance of our personality and essence shifts more towards the essences arising through us. We move beyond our personality defences of separation, allowing presence to unfold in and through our bodies as we become a physical expression of service, right action and healthy relationships. The Presence Essences assist us to be self-aware, to self-care and to self-nourish.

The body is the source through which we experience presence. The key is not to be solely identified with the body or to think the body is all there is. In presence we can go beyond our personalities and our bodies into different states, perspectives and insights. Being beyond our bodies in a presence state is very different than being dissociated out of our body from trauma or distress. We embody best when we are fully in touch with our bodies, mind hearts, souls and spirits. While the body is real, it is not the only truth of who we are.

Healthy embodiment is supported by regularly practising, as well as spontaneously experiencing presence. We learn how to integrate and bridge more skilfully between our inner and outer worlds. We live our daily lives in more expanded, skilful and healthy ways, and we never burn out. One of my favourite writers on embodiment and supporting our nervous systems is Kay Aldred. I particularly enjoy her two books, *Mentorship with Goddess: Growing Sacred Womanhood* (2022) and *Embodied Education, Creating Space for Learning, Facilitating and Sharing* which she co-authored with her husband Dan Aldred in 2023. She and I have an ongoing peer coaching relationship and I have learnt so much from her expertise and neurodivergent way of viewing and interpreting the world

People often ask me how I get so much done in my life and yet never seem stressed or worn out. I am constantly nourished by presence. It is always available, so I never feel depleted. I live in a virtuous cycle of giving and receiving. I constantly receive from presence. My anxiety turns to equanimity so I can thrive within any challenging situation and context. Even though I see suffering all around me and may even experience my own suffering at times, presence helps me to move through it, to cope, and not to be overly anxious or overwhelmed. Presence and the essences keep me in touch physically, emotionally and mentally with what is best in humanity and myself.

Embodying Presence Activism also involves being aware of the impact we have when we engage in action with others. What do people feel or sense when they are with a Presence Activist? What does our specific presence evoke or call forth in others? How can we bring about profound change through being fully present within the realities of climate peril? How can we feel, sense and listen in every moment to discover and discern what is needed next?

A few people choose to be in presence and to live in silence, affecting others with their silent presence. Most of us choose to be present and to live within the world, to have significance, to contribute to society and to make our way financially. Understanding how presence translates into our behaviours, relationships and activism is important.

Presence Activists learn, or already know, how to be kin and to embody the understanding that the world is built on a matrix of relationships where everything is part of a larger flow and that everything exists within a larger context. They experience a genuine knowing in their hearts, minds and souls—that everything is interconnected. They feel oneness and can see what unites.

The aligned Chalice Well Essence for Embodiment is Solomon's Seal which offers "support in those times when you are in conflict and need to find a state of balance and equilibrium to make right choices and decisions."

Presence Embodiment Results

Service

Presence Activism is service from a primary motivation and deep desire to serve by supporting, understanding and empowering others. We know we are not separate, that we are interconnected, and that we can access any or all of the seven essences. We can be in service in every situation. Service becomes easeful and unforced, as our actions are not drained or depleted in any way because they are focused and well supported from the Presence Essences. We are no longer anxious, preoccupied or distracted, and can see clearly what needs to be done. We then take appropriate action that is timely and effective. At the heart of our service, we want those we serve to grow, becoming healthier, wiser, freer, more effective and more likely to be of service to others. Presence Activists don't need to become martyrs or sacrificial lambs.

The Oxford Dictionary defines service as the action of serving, helping or benefiting another, the action of doing something for someone else through acts of assistance, support, healing or kindness. It involves caring deeply about others and being willing to pay attention to their needs. Some people, especially women, can be triggered by the words "servant" or "service," as these words harbor connotations of being diminished or abused. It is important for women to be clear about the differences between genuine service, which comes from a conscious, intentional and liberated place, and sacrifice or servitude. At its best, service flows from the seven Presence Essences which support our capacity, ability and contribution. We are clear about our personal values, virtues and goodness. We gain a deep, overflowing well of loving self-acceptance, and acceptance of others, while achieving tasks and meeting necessary deadlines and outcomes. When centered in authentic service, we can see the connection, unity and harmony of what, at our deepest common purpose, unifies everyone in meaning, purpose and service to each other and the planet.

All faith and wisdom paths have service as a central tenet of living their path in the world.

Seva means selfless service. Seva comes from the Sanskrit root *sev*, "to serve," and is a central concept in Hinduism and Sikhism. The Christian theological virtues of faith, hope and charity were steeped in a sense of service to others. The importance of serving others is articulated in the notion of the stoic, cardinal virtue of katorthoma: the wise person's ultimate way of acting, which involves action based on Divine nature through placing the interests or concerns of others above one's own self-interest. In Islam, zakat is the obligatory contribution of a certain portion of one's wealth in support of the poor or needy or for other charitable purposes. It is one of the five pillars of Islam.

When our service is steeped in Presence Gnosis rather than mind and personality, it becomes truly aligned with a bigger purpose. The well-known prayer of Saint Francis of Assisi, "Lord make me an instrument of thy peace," is a beautiful expression of the notion of service.

As Presence Activists, we ask ourselves "Is there anything I can do to change the situation, improve it, or have a significant impact?" We then take appropriate action from total acceptance of ourselves and others. Our actions are easeful and effortless, without drama. To be in service in presence is to be yourself from the best self you can be in that moment, activating others to their highest self and energetic frequency no matter what their experience of presence may be.

After my 1989 presence experience described in Chapter 2, I knew I could not behave as I had done previously. My toxic personal and workplace relationships and my part in them became clear. Something literally dissolved inside me and I knew I wanted to do things differently. I wanted to use love essence to be of service in life and in my workplace. My specific expression of service, as a leader, is made explicit by Jill Jameson in her powerful book *Leadership in Post-Compulsory Education: Inspiring Leaders of the Future* (2005). She identifies me as a leader whose primary motivation is service. In his doctoral thesis about my work, *Leaders and Spirituality: A Case Study* (2002), Michael Joseph describes how he witnessed my genuine desire to be "of service, to care and love." He witnessed me affecting others by breaking through their mistrust and their previous, negative experiences associated with leaders so that they "felt able to take risks, stick their heads above the parapet and realise more of their potential."

For those of us with privilege, allyship can be conscious activist service for the most oppressed or disadvantaged in society. To ally means to unite or form a connection or relation. Authentic allyship is service and support given by someone from a non-marginalised group who uses their privilege to advocate for a marginalised individual or group. They transfer, in some way, the benefits of their privilege to those who lack it. Being an ally involves significant self-awareness, humility and understanding of others. It involves consistently challenging, unlearning and re-evaluating our own specific position of privilege and power. The purpose of doing this is to support someone else, hopefully alongside a commitment to ending the system of oppression in which we all find ourselves. Being an ally requires deep trust, sensitivity, humility, resilience and a commitment to continual learning. It is a service of supporting and enabling others in ways of which they approve. It is not about offering support and solidarity in a way that isn't helpful, isn't wanted or may harm. That is performative allyship: a situation in which a self-appointed ally wants to receive some kind of reward for being a good person or wanting to be on the right side.

When embodying presence, we no longer have a specific goal or outcome from which anyone can fall short or be made to feel negative or deficient in any way. Such goals no longer serve us.

Through the service of Presence Activism, we embody a presence capacity through which anything that wishes to be brought forward, in service to ourselves and others, can happen purely and directly from the depths of being and presence.

Right Action

For me right action is a skilful, non-violent, calm climate activism steeped in presence. It is a natural and organic embodiment of Presence Activism in which all of our actions have their own, intrinsic rightness and everything we do feels right.

My experience is that when truly in presence, I cannot hurt someone else. Presence transforms us to innately want to live and act from the virtues and to be a benign influence in the world, not for any rewards, simply because that's our state of being. In right action, everything we do is based on wisdom, non-violence and Presence Gnosis rather than our minds and constructed personalities. Our actions are focused, and we see clearly what needs to be done. We take appropriate action that is effective, timely and appropriate to the context. I have always resonated with the Krisnamurti phrase, "clarity is action."

Right action is a Buddhist term which means acting "rightly," without selfish attachment to the outcomes of our actions. We act skilfully and in harmony without causing discord. It is the fourth aspect of the Buddhist eightfold path and involves three main precepts: avoiding all harming of any living being, abstaining from taking what is not given and stopping all abuse of sense-pleasures. It is closely aligned to right livelihood which involves earning a living that does not involve killing, harming, corruption, lying, use of false measures and weights, sexual abuse, selling of alcohol or illegal drugs. As a practising Buddhist for many years, I care deeply about right action and right livelihood, as they describe my relationship to work and activism. I have always tried to make a living through good and honest means and through trying to reduce suffering. I have found working within Further Education, charities, non-profits, community groups and spiritual organisations to be my right livelihood space. Offering Luminary and feminist leadership is also my way of manifesting right action.

None of us know what will happen in the future amidst climate peril. Presence Activists do what we do because we know it is the right thing to do to serve and save our ailing planet. We look at the specifics of the situation and respond accordingly from right action.

The IPPC and numerous other think tanks, summits, gatherings, reports and literature, all offer clear solutions, actions, awareness and information. The world knowscollectively, from a wide range of perspectives, what needs to be done. The self-interest, successful lobbying and anti-climate science responses from significant corporates and the fossil fuel industries—the climate power blockers—are deliberately preventing any sort of systemic and mass change. They unashamedly exhibit "wrong action," over and over again. Some climate activists talk about the gap between having the information and acting appropriately, the "climate action deficit." Both climate power blocking actions and climate action deficit are conscious choices of wrong action in my view.

Recent national and international responses to the global COVID pandemic and the Ukraine War have been swift and effective because they were immediate threats. Climate peril is more diffuse in many countries, so action is not focused upon until emergencies are declared. The Global South is suffering devastating effects right on their doorstep. Moments of crisis, such as world wars, pandemics as well as huge tragedies have brought about a period of significant, systemic change. This hasn't happened yet regarding climate change. How do we move more people, especially key influencers to act? Presence Activism means we are compelled to act and to be of service.

I now focus on practical ways in which we can manifest right action in the world. I believe that the seven actions below will have the most significant impact on both a collective and individual level.

1. Reducing methane.
2. Stopping deforestation.
3. Restoring degraded land, and preventing it from being turned to agricultural use.
4. Changing agriculture and the way we eat.
5. Increasing solar and wind power.
6. Investing in energy efficiency.
7. Stopping the burning of coal.

Individual Right Action

There are many actions that individuals, particularly those of us in the more affluent nations of the world, can take in our day to day lives. I am of the view that if every single individual in the world awakens and acts to alleviate climate peril, then major transformation on a group, community, organisational, national and global level will occur. We can each play our part in saving our beautiful planet, creating change and making life better for everyone. We can influence people and take actions that will make a difference, however large or small. We can advocate, protest and take direct action.

Presence Activists place the climate peril at the heart of all our actions and decision making.

Many books have been written on climate action. You can find numerous climate "to-do lists" online ranging from the tiniest everyday actions through to climate strikes and protesting. Each of us needs to reduce our carbon footprint as much as possible. I provide references and tasters from several sources for you to delve deeper into what you choose to do as a Presence Activist.

I recommend Daisy Kendrick's book, *The Climate Is Changing, Why Aren't We?* (2020), especially Chapter 5, "It's a Lifestyle, Not Just a Movement." In this chapter she provides comprehensive ways in which we can change our everyday lifestyles. She reminds us that between 60% and 80% of our impacts on the planet come from household consumption.

Another book full of practical suggestions of actions you can take is *The Future We Choose: Surviving the Climate Crisis* (2020) by Christiana Figueres and Tom Rivett-Carnac. They suggest ten actions: letting go of the old world, facing your grief while holding a vision of the future, defending the truth, seeing yourself as a citizen instead of as a consumer, moving beyond fossil fuels, reforesting the earth, investing in a clean economy, using technology responsibly, building gender equality and engaging in politics.

Other useful suggestions are provided by the United Nations which describes sixteen actions that individuals can take immediately to reduce their carbon footprints in their paper "16 ways to take action on climate."[40]

Mikaela Loach, in *It's Not That Radical: Climate Action to Transform Our World* (2023), feels that all forms of action to build a better world really matter, from gluing yourself on high profile protests, to making tea and doing administration behind the scenes. She believes that no action is too small, as every action, especially direct action, contributes. She has formed the opinion that real change can only come from outside the system. She proposes both tactical and systemic actions, including joining a trade union, supporting strikes, advocating for climate debt to be addressed and supporting the Global South debt to be cancelled. She also suggests building support and power in our communities through individual actions that form part of community resilience.

Some of the most effective things I suggest we all do to fight climate peril as individuals, include: save energy at home, walk, bike or take public transport, go vegan, eat more vegetables, eat less meat, throw away less food, reuse, repair and recycle, switch to renewable energy in your home, use minimum energy, switch to an electric vehicle travel and reduce non-essential travel, especially air travel. Recycle and keep things in use for as long as possible instead of buying new goods, buy less and when possible, buy locally produced goods to minimise the distances the goods have to travel. You can also buy from sustainable sources or grow some of your own food. Other small yet significant actions include using your own water bottle or mug instead of disposable ones, using efficient light bulbs, turning off lights more often, lowering your thermostat, not selecting one day shipping for online shopping, reducing your use of plastic, unplugging appliances, only buying personal care products that are non-polluting and saving water as much as you can. Changing any excessive consumerist habits is also important.

Across a broader front, you can get involved in influencing the political process at the local, national or international levels or through participation in a climate protest movement. You may prefer to set up or join local green initiatives such as reclaiming land, growing food and feeding people. Organising local Peoples Assemblies on climate issues can be fun, as well as important as is setting up support groups and eco leadership initiatives. You can use your vote based on environmental issues to influence elected politicians and local councillors to ensure they play an active role in politically mitigating climate peril and biodiversity loss.

Try expressing your creativity publicly through visual arts, suggesting ways of making your workplace or school more environmentally friendly, volunteering or campaigning. You could donate to green, environmental charities set up to combat climate change or join environmental protest groups. As a grandmother, I think supporting young people, especially those who are climate activists, is important.

While it is undoubtedly helpful for each of us to take whatever action we can to combat climate peril, individual actions are unlikely, on their own, to solve the wide range of problems, especially the systemic ones. Carbon footprints of individuals are unevenly distributed, the average carbon footprint of someone living in the US is many times greater than someone living in Burkina Faso. This inevitably means that action taken in the US and Europe is much more significant (not better) than action taken in the developing world. Greenhouse gas emissions per person also vary greatly among countries. In the US, emissions in 2020 (the latest available data) were 14.6 tons of CO_2 equivalent per person: more than double the global average of 6.3 tons and six times the 2.4 tons per person in India.

The best we can do, as individuals, is enough. Do whatever you can. While doing everything we can as individuals, we should never let the real culprits off the hook—the corporates, especially fossil fuel companies—as they are responsible for most of the carbon emissions on the planet.

Collective Right Action

The timescale for individual actions to have significant impact is overly long, so major, large-scale, collective action is vital. Making changes on national and international levels has a much bigger impact than individual action.

Getting involved in collective changes that positively impact carbon emissions or improve the resilience of your local community is important. I believe that local collaboration and action are significant ways to combat adverse climate impacts and tipping points that are already apparent and will continue to grow in number and severity. Every form of collective in every country, including corporates, public sector organisations, governments, local councils, charities, voluntary and community groups, needs to embrace innovative, local, national and community-based solutions to environmental and energy problems if we are to meet net-zero deadlines.

Roger Hallam, one of the co-founders of Extinction Rebellion, has stated that a relatively small number of people working together can change the collective consciousness. Bill McKibben, a leading climate campaigner and founder of 350. org,[41] argues that the most important thing people can do is come together to form movements, or join existing groups, that can collectively "push for changes big enough to matter." He sees city-wide renewable energy programmes through to large-scale divestment from fossil fuels.

Caroline Lucas in her New Statesman article, "Why communities are vital to tackling the multiple crises we face: Radical local policies can build the Green New Deal (2023)," says that "only the radical now looks reasonable."[42] She emphasises the need "to harness all the skills, expertise and resources in every corner of the country" to tackle the "polycrisis" of "a climate emergency, cost-of-living scandal, energy crisis and constitutional dilemma" within the UK.

Corporate influencing is fraught with resistance to and denial of climate peril and rife with fossil fuel and corporate self-interest. Yet collective actions by corporates can provide significant and fruitful methods to reduce carbon emissions. Disgustingly, they have used a variety of methods, drawing upon their vast financial resources, to deny or discredit legitimate climate crisis reports and findings that they didn't like or that threatened their profits. They have funded misleading "climate science" and have consistently lobbied international climate change efforts to slow down actions to reduce carbon emissions. They have also tried to shift responsibility away from themselves and onto the individual. This is all out of greed and self-interest to protect their own corporate profits. This is well documented by Michael Mann in *The New Climate War: The Fight to Take Back Our Planet* (2021), and is referred to in speeches by the Secretary General of the United Nations. Shell has been taken to court by climate activists for its irresponsible business strategy.

Governments must also play their part. Governments, unlike individuals, can influence things through legal and regulatory frameworks and via their taxation and spending policies. Unfortunately, many governments have lacked the urgency necessary to deal effectively with climate issues within viable timescales. Delays in taking action are often the result of more immediate, urgent, day-to-day emergencies, underfunding, a lack of political will and a failure to comprehend the seriousness and complexity of climate peril.

On a brighter note, many national and local governments and cities are now signed up to some version of net zero. Ambitious national targets and incentives, which support local action, are being implemented in many countries. France obliges new buildings to have solar or natural roofs, in Denmark and Netherlands new developments are barred from being connected to the gas grid. In the US, National Green Deals involve a combination of robust, top-down policies on green issues, alongside localised power-generation, food and transport schemes.

An important way forward is through genuine, localised, communal decision-making on funded schemes with governments equitably distributing resources and decentralising decision-making power. Taking local agency will be more and more important, especially if societal collapse predictions come true. I chair the Glastonbury Town Deal, a £23.6 million investment from the national government to be delivered locally by March 2026.[43] We hope also to encourage benevolent corporate and philanthropic investors to get involved in a wide range of new eco-projects in Glastonbury stimulated by the initial £23.6 million.

Our grassroots projects are initiated and led by the community. Everyone involved takes green issues and reducing the carbon footprint seriously. Our individual and collective commitment to acting on climate issues is unassailable. Together we are bringing a new energy and synergy to the town to tackle climate emergency. As a community, we are adapting and innovating locally to be as sustainable as we can be.

We are restoring parts of our local Glastonbury community through eleven funded projects to ensure clean energy, regenerative farming, pathways for walking and cycling, a well-being centre, vocational skills training, renovation of old buildings, enhancement of spiritual sites, supporting business, enterprise opportunities and improving sports facilities. We are growing organic food, lowering our carbon footprint, expanding the use of green energy, restoring old buildings and fostering local community building for sustainability. We are also funding thirty places for those who prefer not to live in brick-and-mortar houses and want unconventional, low-impact living in rural surroundings. One of my passions is to find radical, new solutions to solve the housing crisis. I am personally investing in new ways in which my local community can provide eco-homes through community land trusts.

This work is supported by Glastonbury Town Council who in 2019 declared a climate emergency and pledged to be carbon neutral by 2030. It is also currently a majority Green Party council working on five key areas of cutting out waste, switching to renewable energy, supporting nature, sharing experience and expertise and preparing for the changes ahead.

Somerset Council, the accountable body for the Glastonbury Town Deal is committed to tackling climate change and is working towards a carbon-neutral Somerset by 2030.

There are many exciting, innovative, collective projects happening worldwide. I name a few of my favourites. There is an initiative called Village101 in East London. Transition Towns is an exciting initiative with significant work going on in various places around the UK. In my own village, Plotgate, a leading edge community farm produces weekly boxes of vegetables grown on ten acres of land, as well as rewilding many more acres. In August 2022, Faith In Nature, an eco-company of beauty products, became the first company in the world to appoint nature to its board.[44] They recognise what they call the "legal Rights of Nature within our structures." They intend to make responsible board decisions that take the natural world into account, and they have appointed a board director who represents the interests of nature, all species and the environment. They changed their board objects clause to allow the company to have specific regard to nature. They are the first board to do this. I really like it and will be exploring the possibility for boards on which I serve.

Ole Fogh Kirkeby, in *Management Philosophy: A Radical Normative Perspective* (2000), refers to the synchronous and healthy rhythm of a community co-created through the interconnection of many presences. Presence shapes collective situations, transforming what emerges and happens through attentiveness to oneself, to others and to the field of presence. It also involves managing any reactivity, behaving skilfully, valuing everyone involved and encouraging the inclusion of multiple viewpoints. Presence contributes a positive difference in the life of any activist campaign, organisation or community. I am fascinated by the collective field of presence co-created in groups and the skill of holding emergent space for the highest potential of the collective to unfold. I teach and co-create collective presence "fields" as part of my service and activism.

Healthy Relationships

Practising presence is an important part of co-creating resonance and healthy relationships. I believe that everyone wants to feel a sense of belonging and contribution, to be in loving relationships and to be truly seen. Taking the time to be present with others can make us curious and leads to the sharing of deeper and more authentic connection. Healthy and effective partnerships are the way forward for all forms of activism, especially Presence Activism. The Presence Impacts and Presence Results support us in co-creating healthy relationships. Brianna Craft, in her memoir *Everything That Rises: A Climate Change Memoir* (2023), writes about the unhealthy relationships occurring at the climate summits she has attended. She works with the United Nations' Least Developed Countries Group (LDCG). She describes unhealthy relationships between rich and poor countries, an inability to work effectively with consensus and the primacy of national self-interest in a global crisis that can only be solved through cooperation, partnerships and service. Everyone is working to the lowest common denominator instead of the best possible right action. She describes how consensus-based decision-making means that what is agreed must be something that no country will object to, "so it doesn't match the scale of the emergency we find ourselves in." At the same time, those who are responsible back out of pledges, make false promises, walk away and don't deliver. I believe that cooperation, consensus, negotiations and agreement at all the international climate summits, including the annual COPs, are essential for things to move forward quickly. In healthy relationships countries will put aside their differences to solve the climate emergency and governments will collaborate effectively for the forthcoming COP28 meeting in Bonn. It is time for key influencers to find sufficient emotional intelligence, sense of genuine service, bridge building, right action and desire for effective partnerships to ensure the necessary outcomes to save the world.

It is time to move beyond the conflict between rich and poor nations over loss and damage compensation for the most severe impacts of climate disaster in the global south. People in developing countries are feeling increasingly angry and victimised by the climate crisis because rich countries are not responding well. If country representatives at these gatherings took time to be in presence together, I have no doubt that things would move forward very quickly and the Global South would receive the justice it deserves.

In April 2023, The Extinction Rebellion Big One protest with over 60,000 people, was an extensive exercise in coalition building of more than 200 organisations. The four-day protest was a focal point for a broader coalition of activists to work together to protest more effectively against climate change.

As an activist, I believe forming healthy relationships, partnerships and networks is vital. Holding clear boundaries through which we can empathise and support our chosen cause while keeping in touch with our own relationship needs is also important. Presence within collective situations has a palpable power that can be felt by everyone involved, enabling them to feel into their own presence and power. A subtle sense of healing can be communicated simply through the presence field of groups supporting each other's concerns and interests. Our presence can assist others to access presence in group situations. We can literally be Presence Activators, as well as Presence Activists. You might want to revisit the Presence Transmission section in Chapter 1, which is relevant to understanding the impact of presence on other people. Every aspect of our presence has social meaning, and the nature of our presence is the outward reflection of our inner world.

Another key skill of activism is to engage others. Engagement is the extent to which people feel involved with, and passionate about, their purpose in the world, how much they are committed to a campaign or protest and how much they will give their service and their discretionary effort and energy. The level of our own engagement will influence the engagement of others. The more we are genuinely engaged, the more our relationships will flow. Emotional connection through presence encourages motivation and commitment. It is also important to understand what people most care about, what they want to influence and what enables them to feel a sense of belonging and contribution. True engagement cannot be forced, only fostered.

Chaos, complexity, climate anxiety, constant turbulence and challenge can generate a feeling of being unable to relate well to others. Anxiety can make us withdraw and self-isolate. Even if we cannot change or ameliorate external circumstances, we can always choose our responses, attitudes and behaviours by pausing and becoming present. Our capacity to respond with love and trust essences is much greater if we are present, authentic and open-hearted. The more we love and accept ourselves, the more we can do the same for others without any sense of resentment or limitation. The word "responsibility" means the ability to respond: response-ability. We show respect to others by responding to them as fully and as quickly as we can. When we are present in an authentic manner, we are able to respond more appropriately to whatever happens in any group situation, however challenging, easy or unexpected. We can access the strength and resilience essences that allow us to be strong and flexible, as well as responsive to others.

Ole Fogh Kirkeby, in *Management Philosophy: A Radical Normative Perspective* (2000), refers to presence as a "merger with oneself" that dissolves the distance between us and someone else, generating harmony and interconnectedness, effortless flow, rhythm, attunement and awareness aligned with their presence. In all kinds of relationships knowing the right questions to ask and fostering genuine mutual inquiry is far more important than believing we have all the right answers. When we are fully in presence and our attention is focussed on the here and now in our interactions with others, we can give them our pure and undivided attention. We can suspend any judgement or anxiety and take the time to absorb and consider the ideas and feelings of others.

Connection involves emotional intelligence and relational qualities of the heart, including empathy, compassion, deep listening and awareness of your impact on others.

Healthy relationships are all about trust and working together on any issues or challenges that arise. We all impact the emotional states of people around us positively when we can adjust emotionally with the energy and rhythms of individuals and groups. Empathy is the ability to feel what others feel, understand what others have to say and tune in to subtle social signals about what others need or want, understanding, accepting and recognising how someone else is feeling. People with empathy are more able to support others. It is important to learn how to balance deep empathy with getting things done and deadlines met.

***

I hope my suggestions support you in embodying your Presence Activism, individually and collectively. It is important that we all do our best, knowing that every action, however large or small, really does matter. Presence is the most important factor in being a skilful climate activist today, doing our inner work and learning to live and savour every moment.

In the next chapter I explore the Presence Illumination Impacts and Results.

Chapter 7

Presence Flower Illuminations

***

"In the past, changing the self and changing the world were regarded as separate endeavours and viewed in either or terms. That is no longer the case." **Joanna Macy**

***

Introduction

In this chapter, we explore the Presence Flower Impact of Illumination and the Presence Flower Illumination Results of Interconnection, Senses of Self and Views of Reality.

One thing that the threat of climate peril can do is create deep inner questioning and confusion so that we begin to challenge everything we know, including the views we hold about the nature of reality and maybe even the very nature of who we are.

The Presence Flower is a guide and pathway through which we can have profound Illumination and perceive more expansive views on the nature of reality, and significant changes in how we experience reality. Illumination also supports us to understand our sense of self more profoundly and to answer the question, "Who am I?" beyond our ordinary, personality-bound limitations. It helps us to see the interconnection of ourselves with everyone and everything.

Presence informs and transforms the paradigm from which our activism flows. Many things are impacted and change when our personality restrictions and fixations relax sufficiently, when we see multiple realities, when we know the truth of interconnection. The seven Presence Essences manifest and enable such illuminations.

If you are content with your activism, life, personality, current view of reality and senses of self, please stay with them. If you are interested in a significant shift in your life, continue with this chapter. I am offering you the information I wish I had for my presence journey in the 1990s.

I ask you to keep an open, spacious, curious, receptive mind; an open, loving heart; an active intuition and an acute perception of what arises in your body as you read the next sections.

The only way that deep and genuine experiences of presence can occur is through you having them for yourself, directly. Reading, thinking about and gaining insight on presence are useful and important; they will not all affect you to the same extent. It is the practice of relaxing and our direct, visceral experiences that enable us to go beyond our constructed personalities and familiar views of reality, to go beyond the familiar mind, language, thoughts and concepts.

Presence Illumination Impact and Results

To support you in understanding the underpinning Illuminations of Presence Activism, I now describe the Presence Flower Impact of Illumination, then the Illumination Results of Interconnection and finally the different Views of Reality and expanded Senses of Self. These are illustrated in figure 4 below to remind you of their place in the Presence Flower.

Presence Illumination Impact

In the Presence Flower, Illumination involves understanding how our perception is illuminated, changed and expanded by presence. It is the gaining of new insight or experience through feeling illuminated— seeing things differently through having light shone on them. We begin to understand that we are all interconnected, we maintain different views of reality and we have different senses of self.

Illumination involves light, the act of bringing something into the light, of seeing things in the light and having light shone on a subject. For a person, it can include having the quality of light, being a source of light. Words associated with illumination include radiance, transfigured, shining, luminosity, glow and shimmering. Common expressions we use are, "having the light shone on someone or something," "seeing the light" or "having a light-bulb moment."

During the experience of presence, some people report being filled with light, being light or of giving off light. There are many reports of people saying that they have seen someone emanating light.

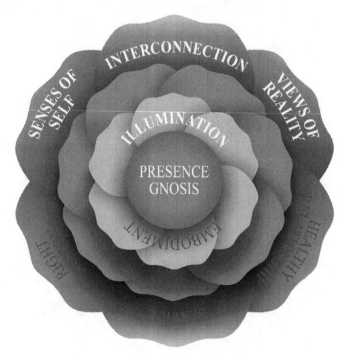

Figure 4 Presence Flower Illumination Impact and Results

I have had numerous experiences of light. I felt, as a teenager, that I was being filled with light when I would spend time in silence or reading sacred literature. After a very powerful, one-month retreat in the Skyros centre in Greece, when I returned home to the UK, people would say that they could see light around me. It was quite an unnerving and interesting experience for me. I have also seen light around others, especially some spiritual teachers.

I spent seven days in a Brahma Kumari ashram in India. The presence of Dadi Janki and Dadi Prakashmani was so strong that I could see bright white auras around both of them. At one point they both seemed completely radiant, aglow and made of pure white light. I have never seen auras before or since. The awesome sunrises and sunsets of Mount Abu enhanced the constant feeling of light within and all around me. I understand then how illumination can be enhanced in conducive environments such as temples, ashrams, monasteries and beautiful landscapes.

All spiritual and wisdom traditions refer to shifting perspectives about reality and our senses of self when we experience Transpersonal Presence. These illuminations are not in the realm of beliefs, thoughts and mind constructs; they are in the realm of direct gnosis. Our constructed personalities and minds are transformed by presence and the essences. We perceive reality and who we are very differently. Different traditions call this illumined mind, enlightenment or seeing true reality beyond the veils. I have explored and met dozens of wisdom teachers from many different traditions, and I have avidly read many spiritual classics and sacred texts. Studying the presence journeys of others, ancient and modern, has informed my own experiences and understanding of different realities and how presence expands our views of reality.

At the centre of my Goddess Luminary Leadership Wheel (Sedgmore 2021) is the archetype of Illuminatrix: she who owns and expresses her Goddess-inspired brilliance and illuminates others, enabling them to shine and to be their own magnificence through a transparent perception of true reality. This informs and underpins my activism, as well as my Luminary teachings.

The two Chalice Well Essences aligned with Illumination are Purple Allium, which "helps us expand our minds to find inspiration and new ways of seeing," and the Star of Bethlehem of Shine which "helps us to be open to receive and to be radiant."

Illumination Presence Results

Interconnection

Presence Activism acts from a perspective of Interconnection which enables our actions to come from a genuine knowing in our hearts, minds and souls that everything is interconnected. When we cognitively and viscerally know interconnection, we realise that "I am you and you are me." We see through to the connection, unity and harmony of what, at our deepest common purpose unifies everyone together in meaningful ways. We begin to experience the world as an organic ecosystem or web of interconnection in which everyone works together, sometimes beyond any human will or understanding. Other people and nature are no longer separate from us. The rivers, earth, forests and vegetation become part of ourselves. Others are us and everything matters, so we can no longer harm. It's taken me years to see no separation and that everything is sacred, especially the land and nature.

When we can see beyond the suffering of our feelings of alienation and no longer see ourselves as separate, we open up to sincere, life-transforming compassion and empathy. We sensitise to the exploitation, discrimination, destruction, greed, hostility, violence and extreme consumption all around us.

Our focus and priorities alter, and we choose to live our lives differently. We see through our constructed personality and see those oppressive, separating narratives of false boundaries, nationality, race, gender, culture, faith and the unnecessary consumption are not set in stone. We see that other people and nature are no longer separate from us. The rivers, earth, forests and vegetation become part of the self. Others are us; everything matters; we can no longer harm because that I am you and you are me. We lose our need to organise and control all aspects of our lives, to feel safe or to be better than anyone else. We no longer feel threatened by our surroundings. We no longer feel insecure and act in unhealthy ways. We experience the world as an organic ecosystem or web of interconnection in which everyone works together, sometimes beyond any human will or understanding. Our sense of safety and trust increases.

In the Presence Flower, Interconnection dissolves any sense of Separation.

Views of Reality

Presence Activism consciously stems from an illuminated perspective on reality and how we act within it from a deep interconnectedness with the goodness and abundance of the universe. The threat of climate disaster can create a deep, inner questioning and confusion, as we begin to challenge everything we know, including the views we hold on our familiar perception of reality.

I want to introduce you to the possibility of understanding conventional, ordinary or dual reality more fully. I will also describe two more realities, the non-dual or boundless reality and the perspective of totality. Some of you may know these different realities already. For others, they may be new and beyond anything you knew existed.

Expanded views on how we perceive reality form part of the lineages and experiences of wisdoms of every culture and every spiritual tradition all across the world. Many people, past and present, have explored and articulated transcendental, mystical reality. My presence experiences have generated significant shifts in my understanding of the nature of reality. These Illuminations have deeply formed and influenced my experience and understanding of presence over the past thirty years. Presence has catalysed and enabled radical shifts in my perception of and comfort with different views of reality.

In the Presence Flower, Views of Reality dissolve the Inner Critic.

My Views of Reality

I have been obsessed with understanding and experiencing the nature of reality since I was a child. I have enjoyed articulating different ways of seeing reality at different times in my life. In intense meditation, in silence and on retreats I fostered my deepening relationship with presence to explore even more deeply two questions: "What is the nature of true reality?" and "Who am I?" I have undertaken a wide range of spiritually formative activities, including a two-year training as an interfaith minister, a five-year training programme as a spiritual healer, a one-year Benedictine Oblate formation, fifteen years in the Ridwhan tradition and five years training as a priestess. Such formation has kept me centred and has enabled me to articulate presence within my activist, personal and professional life.

The experiences I share here are very precious to me. Presence has catalysed and enabled radical shifts in my perception and experience of the nature of reality. In my doctorate (Sedgmore 2013) I describe my journey through unity, oneness and the void in both academic and poetic form. In this book, I expand upon those experiences and add the perspective of (Almaas 2014, 2017), which I have discovered and experienced since 2014.

My first visceral experience of the nondual perspective through a unity experience was in 1989. This experience was followed, several years later, by two other powerful nondual experiences of oneness and emptiness in 2002 and 2005 respectively. The periods between each of these experiences enabled me to consolidate and integrate their impact and to understand their differences, especially my changed experience of presence. More details of these nondual experiences are included in Appendix I *Chronological Stages, Presence Gnosis, Impact of Presence and Transformation of My Personality.*

Moving into nondual and totality perspectives has enabled me to perceive a clearer sense of multiple realities without my internal structures and constructs, conscious or otherwise, obscuring and constraining the way I respond and what I perceive, especially in my activism.

As a student in the Ridhwan school for the past fifteen years, I have found the psycho-spiritual Diamond Heart teachings of Almaas to be the most profound teachings I have ever experienced. His views on the nature of reality and presence have influenced me more than any other philosophical or spiritual teacher. Almaas has enabled me to see that reality is manifesting itself through us whether or not we believe we can control this phenomenon. When we genuinely understand this, our activism can stem from presence rather than personality.

On an eight-day residential retreat in the US, I received Almaas' radical teaching on the "four turnings," in which he articulates four perspectives through which reality can be viewed, or more accurately, four ways in which reality manifests itself through us. Turning one is the perspective of the dual or ordinary world. Turning two is the perspective of a non-dual or boundless reality. Turning three is the perspective of unilocality. Turning four is the perspective of totality. I focus on turnings one, three and four in this chapter.

You can explore these turnings for yourself in his two books *Runaway Realisation: Living a Life of Ceaseless Discovery* (Almaas

2014) and *The Alchemy of Freedom: The Philosopher's Stone and the Secrets of Existence* (Almaas 2017).

My experience is that different realities are possible and can co-exist, yet we can only see the realities we are able to see until our minds expand beyond rational constraints.

Dual Reality or Ordinary World

We all live in the ordinary world of personality perception, primarily knowing and perceiving through our rational minds, our five senses, our feelings, our reactivity and relationships. This perspective is called dual reality, as within this view we see everything as two. Dual means two and encompasses concepts that are underpinned by opposites such as good and evil, me and you, them and us, right and wrong. In the dual, there is always a separate subject and object. We are trained, from childhood, to see everything and everyone as a separate object or person. The chair is separate from the carpet. You are separate from me. We are taught that we are autonomous individuals who can depend only upon ourselves to make our lives work. We are convinced we are located within separate bodies, and therefore, we always feel apart from others, sensing only the sensations within one's own body. I think only my thoughts and feel my feelings, not yours. This separation feels true to us, as in dual reality our conceptual minds work through differentiation. To function we take on self-images, become a bounded, particular personality and disconnect from presence.

While separation may be a useful construct to navigate our conventional world and lives, it causes problems and suffering if we see it as the only reality. We experience anxiety, fear and suffering, as our personalities only know a separation that feels real and true.

Some of us become able to see through the delusion of separateness because of our experience of presence. We understand that the boundaries between self and other are a construct and not the only truth. It changes everything about us—our view of the world and our relationships with other people, animals and nature.

Even when we have experienced other realities, we still live in the ordinary world. Most people live their whole lives never seeing beyond dual reality. They live full, good and satisfactory lives in this realm of reality. Yet to go completely beyond suffering of any kind, including climate anxiety, we need to see that suffering is a personality construct which we can move beyond, relax and dissolve through the Presence Essences. People live in dual reality by being mostly unconscious of presence in their daily lives. They may begin to have glimpses of presence which stimulate their curiosity.

Nondual or Boundless Dimension

Presence can generate a a huge shift in our inner, subjective perspectives of how reality is, how it is very different from the dual, ordinary, everyday reality. Nondual literally means not two. It is a different perspective of reality in which people have a boundless experience of interconnection, oneness, emptiness, fullness and unity. The term "nondual realisation" is used to describe the insight of moving from feeling a sense of separation to directly perceiving unity and oneness, the nondual. Nondual presence experiences can be experienced by anyone regardless of their belief systems. For some people they bring a lasting shift in their perception and comprehension of reality, and they understand that dual or ordinary reality is not all there is.

At the core of this perception lies the direct experience and gnosis of everyone and everything not being separate. In the nondual state, reality is undivided, infinite and boundless. We see through the delusion of believing ourselves to be separate identities and can see all the constructs we have developed through our personality development. Nonduality involves a state of consciousness in which everything, or everyone, becomes one. There is no subject or object; the subject becomes one with the object.

In many nondual wisdom traditions, the nondual is considered better or higher than the dual. From nondual wisdom traditions, the ordinary or dual world has many names that denote difference or delusion such as samsara or maya. This is a way of articulating the primary delusion of separation within dual reality.

From the boundless perspective, presence takes us beyond everything we think we know through a transformative experience of no boundaries and of not being contained within the physical body and mind. We experience a constant, stable, unchanging, beautiful fabric and underpinning of the whole universe to which we can return again and again through presence. We learn that presence is always available even when we are not experiencing it.

This enables us to live in the everyday world of form, being activists in the world, not trapped in only knowing dual reality. Experiencing the nondual catapults us out of reification and differentiation. We no longer conform only to the conventional, collective view of material reality. Experiences of the nondual transcend our constructed personalities and can only be articulated in hindsight. To articulate, we have to draw upon our conceptual, dualistic mind. From the nondual, we can still see the differentiations of the dual, *and* we can also see that everything is interconnected and not separate. One of the best blogs on nonduality is "Nonduality: The Nondual Nature of Reality (Enlightenment)" by Almaas.[45]

In my experience, we are not able to live in the nondual constantly. As we absorb and integrate nonduality, we move back and forth between dual and nondual perspectives within a lifelong process of absorbing, integrating and embodying both perspectives. Some people chose to live as much as possible in the nondual by setting up ashrams, monasteries, convents, isolated communities or nondual supportive communities. They may need to be out of the ordinary world to integrate and learn how to live from the nondual. Others will attempt to live in the dual from the nondual reality, being in the world while not being of it.

As nonduality and boundlessness become our centre of gravity, we find that we know and understand that we are one with the universe and nature. This transformation changes our perspectives on the nature of the universe and our relationships to activism. This is the perspective that informs Presence Activism differs from most activisms, as it is grounded in acting and perceiving from deep interconnection, oneness and unity. While in the nondual perspective, we cannot harm others. We choose to act from the arising of the seven essences.

Totality

I was preoccupied while writing my Doctorate with the question of how I could live and lead after experiencing several nondual states. Was I moving in and out of dual and nondual? Could I remain in the nondual as a leader and activist all the time? Despite learning much from my doctoral studies and thesis, I still didn't feel I understood what was happening until I read Almaas' fourth turning of totality. He had the answer I was seeking. His perspective took away my preferences and judgements about the dual being better and more desirable. I had felt previously that if I was "really spiritual" I could be in the nondual constantly. I discovered I was carrying a sense of deficiency due to my inability to remain in nondual states throughout my busy days. Despite fears that I would not be able to function in my high-powered job as I journeyed into nondual states, I found myself functioning more and more effortlessly and effectively within my everyday life. Totality liberated me into understanding the importance of being exactly where I was in a non-hierarchical way. I also realised that I could now only view the dual and conventional world through the lens of knowing the nondual reality.

Almaas is an inclusive, innovative and extraordinary teacher in that he knows his teachings are only one part of an immense mosaic of truths and realities that are continually emerging. He has no need to hold an ultimate truth in any way; he lives in the constant unknowing and unfolding of continual revelation. He has articulated the perspective of totality, a reality always manifesting itself according to the experiencer, not from any pre-fixed perception, reality or goal. In totality, dual reality, the personality, the mundane material world *and* the nondual interconnect with each other, dancing together. From this perspective, we see that the nondual/spirit and dual/matter spectra are conceptual polarities created by the mind and that reality is not as constant, stable and unchanging as it may first appear in nonduality. Totality challenges any fixed view and goal of what the nondual is, a concept Almaas calls "nondual fundamentalism." It has taken me a while to understand this. As I understand it, nondual teachers support their students to discover a particular nondual path with a preconceived outcome. This goal is the achievement of a nondual state such as bliss, unconditional love, non-attachment, oneness or emptiness. From the totality perspective, the nondual is another form of realisation and perception of reality, not an end state.

A way in which I experience totality is through a mix of being simultaneously human and boundless, being able to witness and fully accept them both as equal. In totality, everything is presence, so it doesn't matter where we are, in anxious personality or in a nondual, boundless dimension of reality. It all comes down to being fully in presence and being "here now" with whatever is unfolding. In totality, matter and spirit are the same within a constantly dynamic, emerging, creative reality that includes and transcends the nondual and dual perspectives.

A way in which I experience totality is through a mix of being simultaneously human and boundless, simply accepting both. An example of living in totality, for me, is when my husband, John, nearly died because his heart electrics were failing. His pulse had dropped to twenty-one, so he was rushed immediately to hospital. It took two hours and many medical staff, to resuscitate him. Fortunately, he lived because of a pacemaker operation. During the ambulance ride, the resuscitation hours and the surgery, my personality was anxious and frightened. My whole nervous system was on high alert. I felt distraught and overwhelmed at the suddenness of it all. My mind was whirling with anxiety, fear, catastrophe and potential loss. We have lived together for the last thirty years and have a very close, intimate, loving relationship. I managed to compose myself through consciously moving into presence in the ambulance ride to the hospital. I danced between remembering to be present, falling into my anxiety, spontaneously being present, and the Presence Essences arising as I needed them. At all times, I was able to provide John with exactly the support he needed. Everyone in the hospital was kind, helpful and professional. I felt like I was in a healthy relationship with all involved. When I was told John was probably going to die, I reacted emotionally, felt deeply upset and knew that my constructed personality would miss him one million percent. I would grieve his physical loss for many years. I remember going into the toilet, looking intensely in a mirror and being filled with an unwavering visceral knowing that "all is well and will be well." Whatever the outcome of John's illness, I would cope, even with his physical death. Everything in me felt the peace, resilience, trust, love and strength essences arising together. From that point on, I could feel my still point and remained deeply in presence.

I still have a strong sense of liberation through my experience with John's near-death situation. While in presence, throughout the experience, I could accept every aspect of the experience without thinking or feeling that I was accepting them; I just was.

I tried sharing that experience with friends and family, and nobody really got it. It was only my companions in the Ridhwan community who could understand what was happening, and I began to reread Almaas' work on totality with deeper insight and understanding.

When I tried to explain the "all is well and will be well" part to family and friends, especially those who don't have a presence or transpersonal dimension to their lives, they thought I was talking complete nonsense or was in some form of denial or disassociation. While I understand their response, I know that is not what was happening to me. From a totality perspective, everything is benign, well and whole, even the suffering of any remnants of constructed personality that are still undissolved. With no judgement, editing or preference, the dual, nondual, or glimpses of totality arise.

If we can be in totality with climate peril, anxiety falls away within the raw state of liberation, re-experienced in every moment of newness and creative dynamism. It no longer matters what our experience is, as we accept whatever is unfolding from any reality at any time. We move beyond any form of hierarchy, goals or expectations, living in the freedom of every moment. Our experience arises and collapses like a quantum wave that depends on the observer and their vibration. Anxiety is no longer constraining or a form of suffering.

Senses of Self

When we know presence as an abiding centre of gravity, we no longer react from our constructed personalities. We see and understand anxiety as an experience that can be dissolved, something we can move beyond and not be trapped in. We also discover that the unskilful, hurtful actions and behaviours of others don't feel so personal anymore and we can respond from a more skilful place in ourselves.

We can be activists from different Senses of Self. If we are fully present and feel interconnection within nondual or totality perspectives, our actions will be more skilful, precise and aligned than if we are acting from a separate constructed self or from suffering within the dual conventional world. None of these are right or wrong; it all depends on which reality we are perceiving from. Self is a fact of our existence and development. We all need a sense of self for identity, self-reflection and consistency.

The experience of going beyond our ordinary, personality-centered sense of self, with all its limitations and restrictions, has been described for centuries. There is a vast academic and spiritual literature on self, personhood and identity. *The Oxford Handbook of the Self* (Gallagher 2011) summarises and explores theories and studies of self from the disciplines of psychology, philosophy, religion and neuroscience. The questions posed and answered by the different perspectives include: Does the self have a real, ontological existence? What is meant by a "sense of self"? Is the self a narrative construction, a cognitive representation, a linguistic artefact or a neurological induced illusion through illness or mystical experience? Mark Sidents, Evan Thompson and Dan Zahavi in *Self and No Self?* (2011) describe the experiences and dialogues of a group of Western philosophers and scholars of Eastern philosophy. I have found common ground within many wisdom traditions, particularly Christian mysticism, Hinduism, Buddhism and the Diamond Heart School. They all agree that a constructed sense of self, your personality, is what lies at the root of all human suffering and separation. They all agree that liberation and wisdom lie in deep inquiry into the nature of self, moving beyond the constructed personality into more expansive realisations and perceptions of self. The constructed personality perspective provides us with the tools and knowledge to function effectively in daily life. It is the transpersonal experience that enables us to no longer identify with our our core identities with constructed personalities.

Presence has catalysed radical shifts in my perception and in how I understand and realise expanded senses of self, beyond my constructed personality.

In the Presence Flower, Senses of Self dissolve Shadow Personality.

My Senses of Self

I am fascinated by notions of self and the nature of subject and object, as well as the different ways in which I behave or see the world at different times in my life. My senses of self have also been highly pertinent to my spiritual growth and development, as I was continually going through different changes, personality relaxations and ways of seeing the world. They provided a holding framework as I shifted from a dual to a non-dual perspective and to totality.

A key question I enjoy playing with is, Who do I take myself to be in any moment, situation or relationship? When I first heard that question on a Ridhwan retreat, it was a game changer for me. To answer it, I allow whatever arises here now, without judgement or editing, without restrictions or fear, remaining in the deepest presence possible. In presence, we can relax, spontaneously or consciously, all the veils and barriers that keep our personality in place.

When exploring presence, many of my Luminary students naturally begin to ponder on their sense of self.

In my doctorate (Sedgmore 2013), I identified and articulated my different senses of self throughout my life. I have included those senses of self and have introduced new insights in this book. I experience all senses of self as occasions for learning, inquiry and conscious unfolding into a broader range of options and possibilities to live from in any situation. Through my journey and continual inquiry, I have come to see that my personality-based self has no real existence nor substance. Rather, it is constructed— both consciously and unconsciously— through thoughts, beliefs, stories, experiences, self-images and personality structures. Barriers with which I have identified since I was a child and have separated me from presence and my fullest potential. Through my presence practices, studies, meditation and Illumination experiences, I have seen through how my sense of self has changed. The personality structures, fixations, behaviours and reactions have become thinner and thinner, enabling me to see things, situations and people as they really are in that moment, situation or event. Through presence, I now know that self can be more fluid and expansive than I ever imagined. Almaas has assisted me to see that our familiar self usually experiences itself through memories and structures created by past experiences. Yet through presence, self can also see itself directly without veils or obscuration, recognising the self's ultimate truth as a primordial presence beyond all concepts and dualities.

I now share seven different senses of self that I have experienced to help you understand what may happen as part of your Presence Illumination.

They are Constructed Self, Shadow Self, Authentic Self, Unified Self, Oneness Self, No-self and Liberated Self. Your journey is unique; my journey is offered only as a map to support and guide you.

In the Presence Flower, Senses of Self dissolve Shadow Personality.

Constructed Personality Self
To function in the world and to survive, we take on self-images and believe that we are a separate individual disconnected

from presence. From childhood, we create our constructed personality self.

Ego means "I" in Latin and can also be called "personality" interchangeably. I prefer the term personality. We all need a personality structure in order to live, develop, survive, relate to others and to thrive. The constructed personality is a sense of self, a locus of selfhood which we cannot completely get rid of, nor should we. Throughout our lives, we form our personalities through a wide range of experiences. We are shaped by the attention and significance we give to people and events, the degree to which we are loved and held by others and both positive and negative situations and relationships. We react to protect ourselves against trauma, abuse, disappointment, adversity, oppression and neglect. We experiment, succeed and fail. We enjoy, we grieve, we find viewpoints, we take positions and we form opinions. All of this personality formation is designed to ensure our survival, to help us cope with whatever we have to face or endure.

At best, our personalities enable us to thrive with a healthy sense of self through which we act and express who we uniquely are. A healthy personality ensures our emotional, mental and physical well-being.

I do not subscribe to the notion that the personality is our enemy, something to be fought or something we ever completely lose. Many psychological and spiritual traditions talk about "transcending the ego." I much prefer the notion of relaxing the constraints and limitations of our personality so our personalities can continually become more expansive and open to the Presence Essences.

I began to see my own personality limitations and fixations through undertaking therapy and beginning to practice daily, spiritual practices such as chanting, walking labyrinths, studying holy scriptures, contemplative retreats, exploring the Enneagram, body prayer and walking meditation. I spent time in monastic environments, in solitude, in silence and in presence. These all assisted the deconstruction of my personality until I was able to see that my personality has no real existence or substance. Rather, it is constructed through thoughts, beliefs, stories, experiences, self-images and ego structures (both conscious and unconscious) with which I have identified since childhood. My personality is enmeshed in habitual, survival patterns of behaviour which can block experiences of presence. Until I did my work described above, my personality barriers and constraints separated me from presence. As my personality structures, fixations, behaviours and reactions became thinner, I began to see more glimpses of presence.

I am now able to see things, situations and people more clearly in the moment, and I can perceive an unfiltered unfolding in the now without my internal structures and constructs, conscious or otherwise, clouding and influencing the way I respond.

When we are ready, open enough and steeped in presence, our personality relaxes and we can access other senses of self. The filter of personality may always be there, yet it becomes lighter and more transparent. I believe that our constructed personalities will show up as long as there is still something to learn and heal.

Activism from the Constructed Personality Self is a mix of high and lows. We can experience burnout, anxiety and overwhelm as we get depleted from being overly busy.

Shadow Self

As we begin to sense that we have a shadow self, we learn how to see the reactivity and fixations of our personality. We learn how we can make skilful and appropriate responses to whatever life presents. Understanding and working with our shadow selves is a subtle, complex, lifelong process of inquiry to determine whether we are living out of our unconscious shadow or from a healthier sense of self. We have already explored shadow in Chapter 3, so here I focus on how we can work with our shadow selves.

Shadow work has three parts: first, the process of getting to know the various aspects and dimensions of out personality of which we are unaware; second, reclaiming and integrating these disowned parts back into our conscious behaviours, intentions and character; third, allowing presence to dissolve more and more of our shadow selves. I have been doing shadow work for many years and have found it invaluable.

Consciously or unconsciously, we have put certain unwanted thoughts, feelings and behaviours into our shadow bag. Sometimes our energy may burst out uncontrollably and unexpectedly. It may feel as though this energy is in control of us or has no connection with who we really are.

When our core survival needs are met or superseded and we no longer feel threatened, we are able to become more consciously aware of our shadow selves. We notice all the things within ourselves that we have given up or not developed enough, the things we feel are lacking. We see how we are disconnected from presence and the seven Presence Essences when in our shadow selves. We begin to face those parts of us that reside in our unconscious and can only come into our awareness when our personalities are strong and healthy enough to cope with them.

Releasing and dissolving our shadow self increases energy and liberates mentally, emotionally and physically. We become able to access every part of the psyche rather than using energy to repress parts of ourselves that were previously unwanted or unsafe to express. Through healing our shadow selves, we can become the people we were always meant to be. We become skilful and stop behaviours that no longer serve us or anyone else.

Shadow is easier to see in others than in ourselves and is problematic only if we don't explore, acknowledge and understand it. It is important to become really clear about what belongs to you and what belongs to someone else's shadow self.

Activism from this Shadow Self is overly reactive, often discordant and may cause huge suffering for ourselves and others, especially when we act out inappropriately.

Authentic Self

Having a healthy personality makes a big difference, not only in our own lives, but also in the impacts we have on others. Authenticity means living our lives by knowing and being close to the truth of who we are, being fully congruent with our core values and beliefs. In our authentic self, we understand our unique personalities, character traits, charismas and beliefs. Some less desirable aspects of our personalities may always remain, yet we can acknowledge them and understand our limitations. I am still impatient despite having experienced significant presencing in my life while other personality facets of mine have relaxed completely. The difference is I rarely act on my impatience. Now I notice it, pause, then let it go. Our shadow becomes a means of learning and growth rather than self-blame or suffering. A healthy, authentic self can access its highest potential, best behaviours and the natural goodness that exists in all of us.

Personal Presence enables us to live our authentic self through presence. An authentic person feels genuine and enables others to be genuine too. Their integrity is recognised by others and builds trust. Authentic people embrace their ethical values and strengths. They accept and love themselves.

Developing a healthy and authentic personality is enough to last a lifetime for most people. Others choose to continue into deeper explorations. We can go beyond a healthy, authentic and well-developed sense of self and experience presence as a portal to the nondual and more expanded senses of self.

Activism from the Authentic Self is congruent with our values and beliefs and is steeped in right action.

Unified Self

Through this sense of self, we can see who we are beyond our beliefs, patterns, shadows and personality traits. We understand that our constructed, authentic selves are not all that define and express us. Through being in presence, we gradually, or suddenly, move into a very different sense of self. We discover a profound, unshakable, palpable, visceral knowing of union with something more than our personality. We move beyond being a self-contained, separate self.

In the unified self, there is a conjoining of our constructed personality selves in a union of something bigger than ourselves—a unity, surrender and absorption. We experience two being united. We see that the constructed self and the authentic self are no longer the only selves that we are.

My experience of self shifted to uniting with something sacred. My constructed personality self dissolved. I was filled with presence, as well as being united with it. I felt this union as a mystical marriage, filled with Transpersonal Presence that liquefied and softened me in a golden light. It was an exquisite, loving union of myself and the sacred. The name and form of this sacred other, which was no longer separate, has changed over the years. I have experienced it as God, Goddess, Source, Nature and the Divine. For many the unified self is not sacred; it is more of a simple unity with a universal energy or flow.

The unified self brings a transition into nondual reality in which there are no longer two, no separation of any kind. We may fall out of our unified self when we are not in presence, so being in presence as much as possible really helps.

The self we dissolve or give up in unified self is a construct of the mind. Giving this construct up will initially feel like a death, a death of our constructed personality, yet is necessary to eventually experience the unified self as our centre of gravity.

Activism from the Unified Self is a precious, sometimes sacred, offering of service steeped in union, with access to one, several or all of the Presence Essences.

Oneness Self

In unified self, two become one. In oneness self, we realise that there never were two to unite in the first place. Interconnection becomes visceral as we experience ourselves as one with everyone and everything. Some of us experience unified self before oneness of self. Others move directly into oneness without the need for a unified self. I know people born knowing interconnection; some Indigenous cultures imbue it from birth.

In 2002, on an Enneagram workshop, I experienced total oneness rather than unity. I realised there never was any division, no separation anywhere in the universe, there never ever had been two. There had only ever been one. I expressed this in my journal as "being one with all that is, simultaneously seeing *and* being the true reality, fully awake and present without any preconceptions or expectations." In this experience, my constructed personality self, authentic self, and unified self, completely dissolved into oneness. I had a direct, visceral knowing of "All is One," of I am God, Goddess, Source, the Divine. I was presence rather than being filled with presence. I was eternal, timeless, expansive and boundless. I could see even more deeply how my personality was a construct, a sham, and how I had no separate self. All the Presence Essences became available to me in that moment. Nature Presence is frequently a oneness experience.

From the oneness self, we treat others based on seeing them as ourselves: interconnected, interdependent and sacred. We see and relate to others through a sense of virtue and connection rather than morality or good and evil. Practical, daily problems become issues of delusion rather than evil, and any solution lies in not applying our will or moral codes. We have accurate insight about the interconnected nature of all things and people.

Activism from Oneness Self is a selfless service and precious act of interconnection and Kinship.

No-self

This involves being without any self, literally the disappearance of our constructed self. This happens through an experience of emptiness, blackness, nothingness, stillness or spaciousness. Buddhists and other wisdom traditions name this the void, no-self or emptiness. Nirvana in Buddhism literally means to be snuffed out, completely gone. In the experience of no-self we no longer have a sense of self in any kind of conceptualised manner. Pure nothingness or emptiness, rather than oneness or unity, is the core experience of no-self.

I explored and practised Theravadan Buddhism for fifteen years. I first learned how to meditate in this tradition when I was twenty-five. During a one-week Enneagram workshop with Russ Hudson on the Holy Ideas (Almaas 1990), I had my first direct experience of no-self in which time disappeared and I literally experienced emptiness, an empty blackness, of nothing being there. I had gone completely. Paradoxically, there was also a sense of fullness, completeness, stillness and deep inner peace. The words of the Buddhist *Heart Sutra*, which I had read and studied regularly for over twenty years, suddenly revealed their deepest meaning to me, and I understood the meaning of the words, as translated by Pine (2004).

***

> *form is emptiness, emptiness is form;*
> *emptiness is not separate from form,*
> *form is not separate from emptiness;*

whatever is form is emptiness,
whatever is emptiness is form.

***

It was a huge insight. From then onwards, I have experienced directly the truth and reality of both form and no form, the nature of the void and the expansiveness of space as another facet of who I am. I can see my constructed personality as a shell and fabrication of the mind. Everything I have ever known is a construct of the mind, but in that moment of no-self the constructions all disappeared. In no-self, there is only quietness, stillness, formlessness and emptiness at the core of everything, including me. I know that everything arises out of nothing which feels more like an unknowing of all that I had previously thought was true.

No-self has left me with a deeper acceptance of things as they are, being non-attached to things in my ordinary world. I also experience a deeper unfolding of presence and the Presence Essences from spaciousness and emptiness, beyond anything I can ever know with my mind.

No-self was the most difficult experience to allow, as it initially terrified me to let go into this void. It felt like a black hole into which I might disappear and never return. I questioned how I could continue in my professional work and activism if I really let go into this nothingness. Yet what I have found following on from the experience is that I can live a fuller life and have even more success and spontaneity as an activist. This spaciousness enables me to hold an open and expansive space for actions to unfold. I experience an emergence of form (the manifest) out of being centered and aligned with formlessness (the non-manifest) into the world of action. I can now act from any sense of self—no-self, constructed personality, unified self or oneness self—drawing upon whichever is most appropriate.

Activism from No-self flows and unfolds in right action and non-attachment from the spaciousness and unknowing of the void.

Liberated Self

The liberated self is so named because this self is liberated from anxiety, overwhelm, rumination, burdens, expectations, desires or any need to influence and change anything. I only get glimpses of this; it is not my centre of gravity. This sense of self takes us to a new level of being fully open, accepting and aware of whatever arises. It is effortless; striving cannot make this sense of self arise. It happens when it happens. It doesn't hold a position or a preference, easily accessing any sense of self within all perceptions of reality. Whatever the situation in which we find ourselves, we experience perfection. It is what it is. If we have any preference, anxiety or judgement of any kind, then we are not in this liberated self in that moment.

In *The Alchemy of Freedom: The Philosopher's Stone and the Secrets of Existence* (2017), Almaas describes liberation as a condition of freedom, not so much a liberation from oppression, but more so the raw state of liberation itself, so liberating that it doesn't matter what our experience is. We may be joyful or flat, anxious or relaxed, alone or in company, struggling or at ease; any state or sense of self is fine. We are free from anxiety, suffering or struggle. In the liberated self there is no hierarchy of self; each self is valid and appropriate as it arises. We understand that we need our healthy, authentic, constructed personalities to function well in the conventional world. The liberated self no longer prefers or rejects a particular perspective of reality or sense of self. It can experience multiple senses of self simultaneously by being non-attached and moving beyond any fixed position. Being able to access more senses of self is more expansive yet not necessarily better.

I share a significant glimpse of liberated self I experienced during a challenging situation. I have already recounted my husband's near-death experience in the totality section above. A second situation involved half my house burning out. What happened to me on both occasions was an experience of seeing my constructed personality react while experiencing no-self, unified self, oneness self and liberated self, with no clinging or preference to whatever self I was in.

I witnessed the blackness, the acrid smell and internal destruction of half of my house after a serious fire had burnt it out. While my constructed personality experienced upset and trauma, I knew, deep within, that everything was well and always will be well. Initially, I was affected emotionally and aesthetically, and I cried when I walked through the blackness and soot and ash of the fire. Then spontaneously it became the blackness of the void. I had a powerful sense of non-attachment to the house and everything in it even though the fire occurred immediately after completing seven years of building and restoring: a massive labour of love. I also felt a sense of no-self and of the indestructibility of everything, including me, in the midst of the burnt-out blackness.

I had to run a workshop the day after the fire, a quiet day retreat in Glastonbury Abbey House. What is most fascinating to me was that somehow, because of the fire experience, I got completely out of my own way as a facilitator. The day went incredibly well, it flowed with ease, I was non-attached: in deep unity and interconnection with every participant and present throughout the day. At no point did I feel disassociated or in suffering. When closing the day, one of the participants shared a poem by Thomas Merton which drew on the metaphor of losing your house, an extraordinary synchronicity, as I had not mentioned that half of my house was burnt out. I resonated deeply with the poem and shared about my house fire, as it felt appropriate at that point. I remember vividly their kindness, yet I mostly remember their astonishment and gratitude that I had facilitated so well despite a significant fire the day before.

In hindsight, I feel that my constructed, healthy, authentic self had acted out of a genuine commitment, love and service to do my duty and to facilitate the quiet day. It had been planned for a year and people had paid and registered. My unified and oneness selves were in harmony with everyone involved and with the Presence Essences. Everything felt perfect, including what was happening on the material plane, as my liberated self accepted whatever self I was in at any point in the day. I wasn't overwhelmed, stressed or anxious.

Liberation lies in allowing whatever is arising from any sense of self I am in at any moment, not in hanging onto or preferring the continuation of any thought, feeling or sense of self.

I saw that a nondual state was not more of an achievement or a better state to be in than responding authentically from my constructed personality. It is only a human emotion, a release, to cry when your house burns down.

Activism from Liberated Self involves a whole new level of being fully open, accepting and aware of whatever arises. It is effortless. It doesn't hold a position or a preference, easily accessing any sense of self or any perception of reality. We no longer desire to be in any one particular sense of self. Whatever the situation in which we find ourselves, we are in perfection.

***

I hope my descriptions of the Illuminations of Interconnection, different Senses of Self and expanded views of Reality support you in your activism. They are important portals of the Presence Flower. I agree with Almaas in *Runaway Realization: Living a Life of Ceaseless Discovery* (2014): continual and multiple illuminations, realisations and perspectives are possible as long as we are breathing. For me, these Illuminations have transformed my activism and have supported me to live with, and beyond, anxiety while doing my best to be a skilful climate activist.

I conclude with a blessing in the final section.

Presence Activist Blessing

"Respond to the call of your gift and the courage to follow its path." **John O'Donohue**

Thank you for reading this far and completing the book. May this moment be both an end and a new beginning, one of many more beginnings in your journey with Presence Activism.

One of my favourite poems that I read frequently and have shared with many students is "For Presence" by John O'Donohue from his gorgeous book *Benedictus: A Book of Blessings* (2007). In this blessing, he prays that anxiety never lingers about you, that your inner and outer dignity align and you experience wonder. As I read again through his blessings, I see many of the Presence Flower Essences and Impacts expressed throughout the lines in an exquisite and profound way.

May Presence Activism equip and expand you to act and flow skilfully and dissolve your climate anxiety. May you feel ready to face new challenges, to cope better with existing ones and to thrive through whatever frontier and new places you have yet to journey through.

To close, I offer my own presence blessing, written especially for you, precious reader and Presence Activist companion.

Presence Activist Blessing

From the Presence of All that is, is not,
And ever will Be

***

Hold us in
The depth of peace and stillness beyond all understanding
The love that pervades and conquers all
The joy that uplifts through bliss and gratitude
The strength that means we never give up
The trust that fosters connection and community
The resilience through which we persevere
The flow that generates ease and well being

***

From the Presence of All that is, is not,
And ever will Be

***

May Essences flow and fill each and every one of us
Our Presence resounding
Our hearts wide open
Our minds radiating brilliancy
Our wills supporting
Our soul wisdom discerning

***

From the Presence of All that is, is not,
And ever will Be

***

May we be shining lights
Illuminated and illuminating
Knowing and living interconnection
Our senses of self constantly expanding
Boundless and glorious
Beyond all limitations

Being who we truly are in every moment
Free from anxiety

***

From the Presence of All that is, is not,
And ever will Be

***

May we be skilful Presence Activists
Living examples of
Presence personified in right action
Working tirelessly to better the world
Unconditional selfless service
Co-creating healthy relationships
Impacting positively everywhere we are called

***

From the Presence of All that is, is not,
And ever will Be

***

May those who can make a difference wake up
May climate peril be seen and responded to
May Mother Earth be nourished and safe
May all beings live well in their safe habitat

***

From the Presence of All that is, is not,
And ever will Be

***

Amen, Om Shanti, Salam, Shalom and Blessed Be.

About the Author

Dr. Lynne Sedgmore CBE is an activist, executive coach, non-executive board member, priestess, interfaith minister, published author, poet and former chief executive. She has been involved in environmental and feminist campaigns and numerous protests since the 1970s. She bridges mainstream organisations and spiritual communities. She coaches individuals and senior teams in charities and organisations that inspire her. The organisations she led have won numerous awards. She was appointed CBE for services to education and was named as one of the UK's "100 Women of Spirit" and as one of the most influential people in the Debrett's 500 list.

She is the author of *Goddess Luminary Leadership Wheel*; *Enlivenment: Poems*; *Healing Through the Goddess: Poems, Prayers, Chants and Songs*; and *Crone Times: Poems*.

Lynne is active in Extinction Rebellion, she Chairs the Glastonbury Town Deal and she is a Priestess of Avalon within the Glastonbury Goddess community. She is a student in the Ridhwan school of inquiry. She has worked extensively with the Enneagram. Her leadership impact, Luminary teachings and poetry have featured in many books, articles and magazines.

From the Author

Thank you for purchasing *Presence Activism*. My sincere hope is that you derived as much from reading this book as I have in creating it. If you have a few moments, please feel free to add your review of the book to your favourite online site for feedback.

If you would like to connect with me further, please email me on lynne.sedgmore@gmail.com or visit my website at
www.lynnesedgmore.co.uk.

Sincerely,
Lynne Sedgmore

Appendix I

Chronological Stages, Presence Gnosis, Impact of Presence and Transformation of My Personality

In Figure 5 below, I articulate my range of specific experiences in chronological order and describe the impact of presence and its transformation of my personality at different times in my life.

***

Stage	Presence Gnosis	Impact of Presence	Transformation of my personality
Up to 1989 *Journeying TO Presence* *Experiencing my Personal Presence* *Spontaneous Glimpses of Transpersonal Presence*	Mostly aware of my Personal Presence. Living from my familiar personality and dual reality. Understanding my own personality needs and shadow. Glimpses of something bigger, deeper, stiller beyond myself. Very occasionally spontaneously filled with light, stillness and peace.	Others commenting that I have a strong personality and my Presence affects them. Searching for truth, goodness, authenticity and values. Actively exploring my understanding of the Divine. Actively attempting to reform my personality. Able to witness my experiences of suffering, anxiety and anger.	Minimal impact. Steeped In my constructed personality and ego perceptions. Acting and feeling less and less from conscious and unconscious familiar personality constraints, emotional and psychological shadow and constructs. Some suffering alleviated. Increasing self awareness.

Figure 5 Chronological Stages, Presence Gnosis, Impact of Presence and Transformation of My Personality

Stage	Presence Gnosis	Impact of Presence	Transformation of my personality
1989–2004 *I am WITH Presence* *Directly experiencing Presence Essences and as Union with the Divine*	Experiencing a timeless, eternal transcendent Presence as both beyond/ separate, and also within myself. I dissolve into the one-ness of Transpersonal Presence as **two** becoming united. Feeling surrender and absorption. Presence descends on me from a transpersonal source. Recognition of, and desire for the Essences and benefits of Presence.	Wanting to be of service to others. Being the face of the Divine in the world. Wanting to live a virtuous and good life through moral and spiritual character. Wanting to be collaborative with others. Being infused with Presence Essences, especially light and love.	My personality becomes more and more able to access the different Essences. Experiencing a transcendent self. Feeling united with the Divine, as one, in surrender and absorption. I begin to question my personality and no longer feel 100% I am the "me" I thought it was. I begin to notice the Essences as something I "have".

Stage	Presence Gnosis	Impact of Presence	Transformation of my personality
2004-2013 *I AM Presence.* *Directly experiencing Presence as Oneness* *Knowing Non-duality* *Non-conceptual Presence and No-Self, Void and Emptiness*	I know I am one with the Divine, and there never were two. I am the oneness of all forms that exist. I am interconnected, not separate. Spaciousness with no boundaries. I know myself in non-dual reality.	Interconnection with everyone and everything. All the Essences become accessible. Flow and synchronicity. Deeper serenity. Visceral knowing of radical trust. Loss of the sense of Presence of a personal God. A deeper understanding of service, as selfless.	No separation. Directly seeing my constructed personality. Working with my unconscious shadow. Loss of familiar personality and conventional sense of self into nondual experiences of unknowing, boundlessness and spaciousness.

Stage	Presence Gnosis	Impact of Presence	Transformation of my personality
2014-2023 *Abiding in Presence* *Presence as a centre of gravity* *Presence as a constant state beyond practice* *Experiencing Totality* *Being Here Now consistently*	Consistent arising of Essences as needed. Pure presence, beyond all constructs. Absence of deficit. Everyone and everything are palpably Presence. Presence is constant, is everywhere and always there. Unfolding and embodying align and arise from Presence. Letting go and letting come in the emergence of now.	Living simultaneously, with and beyond, personality needs and limitations. Having a clear conscious choice to access the most appropriate Essence. Doing through non doing - Wu Wei. Constant awareness of being Presence while able to act and to be in the world in real time. Being in Selfless Service. Essences arise and flow appropriately as and when needed in any context.	Relaxation and awareness of all personality as constructs. No longer knowing self in a conceptualised way. Experiences of nothingness. Being exactly where I am, in which ever sense of self or view of reality. Total acceptance of here now. Loss of suffering and deficit into liberation. Equanimity in most situations.

Appendix II

The Physiology of Calming Our Nervous System and Brain

You can consciously calm and self-manage your nervous systems. I offer basic information to assist you in doing this. I am not a mental health specialist and I advise any reader who needs therapeutic intervention for their anxiety to go to a therapist who specialises in anxiety, calming your nervous system and the impact of climate peril on individuals.

The autonomic nervous system has two main divisions, the sympathetic and the parasympathetic. I also offer brief notes on the brain and polyvagel theory.

Sympathetic Nervous System

The sympathetic nervous system is responsible for preparing the body for fight, flight, freeze or fawn. These are activated when we become anxious. Our default state is the sympathetic nervous system which is constantly looking for negativity and danger. We do not want to be in a state of sympathetic dominance for extended periods as this can lead to health problems, including high blood pressure, heart disease and anxiety. In the fight response, we go towards fighting the threat to eliminate it. In flight, we move away as quickly as we can. Fawning involves becoming more appealing to the threat by people pleasing, becoming co-dependent or losing boundaries. The freeze response happens when our brain is unable to respond to a threat and we feel able to move away from the threat. We literally freeze by remaining still, unable to move, totally numb.

We may dissociate from our bodies in all these states. They are built-in defence mechanisms that cause physiological changes, including rapid heart rate and reduced perception of pain. These features enable us to unconsciously protect ourselves by releasing endorphins that calm the body, helping to relieve the stress and anxiety. They are all responses to a threatening or dangerous experience that is too difficult to process. Grounding and bringing ourselves into presence can bring us out of a fight, flight, freeze or fawn response.

When our sympathetic nervous system is activated, our amygdala, the emergency-button part of the brain, alerts the hypothalamus to any danger. This activates our neocortex, the rational part of our brain, to ascertain the nature of the threat. Then the hypothalamus readies our body to respond by triggering the release of the stress chemicals adrenaline and cortisol. Adrenaline makes our hearts beat faster to pump oxygen to the brain to help us to think, plus we can hear, feel and smell better. Our breathing speeds up and our lungs open more to absorb the increase in oxygen and to feed it into our bloodstream. Simultaneously, some of our fat and glucose supplies are mobilised, providing extra energy to fight or flight. Cortisol is released while any perceived threat is still possible, this keeps us physically on high alert, so we do not become harmed or complacent. All of this is designed to keep us as safe as possible from danger or threat.

Parasympathetic Nervous System

We are at our best when we live from the parasympathetic part of our nervous systems, an important part of the body's autonomic nervous system which informs our brains as to what is happening, helping us to feel safe and connected to other people and to nature. It controls and supports the body's ability to relax and down regulate, helping us to maintain a healthy resting heart rate, metabolism and breathing rate after any threat has passed.

Presencing stimulates and increases the parasympathetic nervous system activity which returns our body to a state of rest and digest, signaling to our body that there is nothing to be anxious about.

This reduces stress and promotes relaxation. It also lowers our heart rate, blood pressure, breathing rate and muscle tension.

We have a robust nervous system if it gets stimulated and then calms down easily afterwards, without us having to think about it or attend to it. The ability to move between the sympathetic nervous system enables us to manage reactivity and arousal so that we can move and respond to things without being so anxious. Physiological health and emotional well-being are enhanced by being able to move consciously between these two nervous system states readily, easily and quickly. Self-regulation involves developing the skill of choosing which state we want to be in. We can learn to reroute our more primitive reactions to reduce anxiety, drawing on presence.

Another major player in this calming process is the vagus nerve, a cranial nerve that carries thousands of sensory fibres that create a pathway that interfaces with the parasympathetic control of the heart, lungs and digestive tract. It sends signals from the brain to the body and vice versa through the nerves. Stimulating the vagus nerve helps to calm anxiety and manage our nervous systems. It runs from the brain to the abdomen sending information on the state of our organs to our brains. This matters because the brain informs the body on how to keep functioning. Ways of stimulating the vagus nerve include breathing exercises, cold water exposure, humming, chewing gum, yawning, gargling and singing, meditation and presencing.

Polyvagal Theory

Polyvagal theory was developed by Stephen Porges and articulated in *Polyvagal Safety: Attachment, Communication,*

Self-Regulation (2021). He identifies a third type of nervous system response, the social engagement system that plays a role in our ability to socially engage, or not. Porges' theory views the parasympathetic nervous system as being split into two parts, a ventral vagal system that supports social engagement and a dorsal vagal system that supports immobilisation behaviours. He advocates a mix of activating and calming to strengthen our nervous system if it is arrested or has been dysregulated by trauma. He proposes pendulum exercises to intentionally bring ourselves out of relaxation into light stress and then back into a safe state. The oscillation trains the nervous system to calm and relax more quickly. I know people who have found this approach invaluable.

The Brain

Our brains are the interface between the inside and the outside, an energy system, always learning and responding to our environment. The brain is the most complex system in the universe. In relation to anxiety, it is important to understand that our brains are always learning and actively responding to the environment and to presencing. They are what is termed plastic, constantly rewiring with new neural connections being formed and re-formed all the time. Our brains constantly enable new behaviours. Even the most entrenched behaviours, including anxiety, can be modified at any age. This explains why developmental, therapeutic, spiritual disciplines and practicing presence are all very important. We can significantly change our brains, thereby changing our behaviours and levels of anxiety.

In *The Neuroscience of Leadership: Harnessing the Brain Gain Advantage*, brain scientist Jeffrey Schwartz (2006) explains how neural connections can be reformed, new behaviours can be learned and even the most entrenched behaviours can be modified at any age. This is good news for anyone wanting to relieve their climate anxiety. Yet the brain will only make these shifts when it is engaged, reflective, serene and focussed. In a threatened state, people are much more likely to be "mindless." Their attention is diverted by the threat, and they cannot easily move to self-discovery or awareness. People who feel betrayed, threatened, unrecognised or diminished experience these as a neural impulse, as powerful and painful as a blow to the head. Tali Sharot, in *The Influential Mind* (2018), explains how our brain is wired to respond to positive information and the potential of achievement with a "go response" when we are not anxious.

Online Resources

Introduction

1 "Intergovernmental Panel on Climate Change," *IPPC*, May 6, 2023, https://www.ipcc.ch/.

Chapter 1 The Context of Climate Peril

2 Damian Carrington, "Ecosystem collapse 'inevitable' unless wildlife losses reversed," *Guardian*, February 24, 2023, https://www.theguardian.com/environment/2023/feb/24/ecosystem-collapse-wildlife-losses-permian-triassic-mass-extinction-study?CMP=Share_iOSApp_Ot.

3 "Tell the Truth," Extinction Rebellion, accessed April, 26, 2023, https://extinctionrebellion.uk/the-truth/.

4 Jem Bendell, "Deep Adaptation: A Map for Navigating Climate Tragedy," (online), 2020, http://lifeworth.com/deepadaptation.pdf,59.

5 Jem Bendell, "After Climate Despair — One Tale Of What Can Emerge," January 14, 2018, https://jembendell.com/2018/01/14/after-climate-despair-one-tale-of-what-can-emerge/.

6 Jem Bendell, "Hope and Vision in the Face of Collapse: The 4th R of Deep Adaptation," January 9, 2019, https://jembendell.com/2019/01/09/hope-and-vision-in-the-face-of-collapse-the-4th-r-of-deep-adaptation/.

7 Guy McPherson, accessed May 8, 2023, https://guymcpherson.com/.

8 Sam Carana, "Artic News," accessed April 19, 2023, http://arctic-news.blogspot.com/.

9 James Hansen, "Realistic Path to a Bright Future," online, December 20, 2021, http://www.columbia.edu/~jeh1/mailings/2021/BrightFuture.03December2021.pdf.

10 Iddo Landau, "5 Ways in Which the World Has Been Dramatically Improving Think the world is deteriorating? Think again. We have reasons to be pleased," November 15, 2018, [https://www.psychologytoday.com/intl/blog/finding-meaning-in-imperfect-world/201811/5-ways-in-which-the-world-has-been-dramatically.

11 Julius Probst "Seven reasons why the world is improving," January 10, 2019, https://www.bbc.com/future/article/20190111-seven-reasons-why-the-world-is-improving.

12 Jem Bendell, "Hope and Vision in the Face of Collapse: The 4th R of Deep Adaptation," online, January 9, 2019, https://jembendell.com/2019/01/09/hope-and-vision-in-the-face-of-collapse-the-4th-r-of-deep-adaptation/.

Chapter 2 Presence

13 Claire Ratinon "When the climate crisis brings despair, I cultivate my inner connection to nature — and find hope," *Gaurdian*, accessed May 8, 2023, https://www.theguardian.com/commentisfree/2023/mar/01/bumper-blossom-buds-garden-hope-natural-world.

Chapter 3 The Presence Flower

14 Presencing Institute, website, accessed April 19, 2023, https://presencinginstitute.org/.

15 "Chalice Well Flower and Tree Essences," *Chalice Well Trust,* accessed June 4, 2023, https://www.chalicewell.org.uk/webshop/chalice-well-essences/.

16 T. S. Eliot, "1. Burnt Norton," *Four Quartets,* online, Accessed April 19, 2023, https://www.poetryverse.com/ts-eliot-poems/four-quartets-burnt-norton.

17 Jem Bendell "Deep Adaptation: A Map for Navigating Climate Tragedy," online, July 27, 2020, http://lifeworth.com/deepadaptation.pdf, 59.

18 leadershipembodiment, "Introducing Leadership Embodiment," *YouTube,* October 25, 2012, https://youtu.be/jbCDOmrds0Y.

19 Brian Draper, "Talking the Walk, an Interview with Satish Kumar," *High Profiles,* September 3, 2013, https://highprofiles. info/interview/satish-kumar/.

Chapter 4 Presence and Climate Anxiety

20 "Word of the Year 2019," *Oxford Languages,* accessed June 1, 2023, https://languages.oup.com/word-of-the-year/2019/.

21 "Nurturing the Fields of Change," *Alef Trust,* accessed April 19, 2023, https://www.aleftrust.org/alef-applied/nurturing-the-fields-of-change-programme/.

22 "The Climate Change Anxiety Scale," *Emerge,* accessed April 19, 2023, https://emerge.ucsd.edu/r_1otfxsqqgiayc80/.

23 "The Climate Anxiety Scale (CAS)," *Frontiers,* accessed April 19, 2023, https://www.frontiersin.org/articles/10.3389/fpsyg.2022.870392/full.

24 Gregory Andrew, "Eco-anxiety': fear of environmental doom weighs on young people," *Guardian,* accessed April 10, 2023, https://www.theguardian.com/society/2021/oct/06/eco-anxiety-fear-of-environmental-doom-weighs-on-young-people.

25 Bath University (2023) "Climate Action Survey," *Bath University,* March 15, 2023, https://blogs.bath.ac.uk/climate-action/2023/03/15/climate-action-survey-results-2023-students-and-staff-united-to-drive-strong-action/.

26 "Stress in America, A National Mental Health Crisis," *American Psychological Association,* accessed April 19, 2023, https://www.apa.org/news/press/releases/stress/2020/report-october.

27 Caroline Hickman, Elizabeth Marks, Panu Pihkala, Prof Susan Clayton, R Eric Lewandowski, Elouise E Mayall, Britt Wray, Catriona Mellor, Lise van Susteren "Climate anxiety in children and young people and their beliefs

about government responses to climate change: a global survey," *Lancet Planetary Health,* 5, no. 12, (December 2021): e863-e873, https://www.sciencedirect.com/science/article/pii/S2542519621002783.

28 David Wallace-Wells, "When Will Climate Change Make the Earth Too Hot for Humans?" *New York Magazine,* accessed June 2, 2023, https://nymag.com/intelligencer/2017/07/climate-change-earth-too-hot-for-humans.html.

Chapter 5 Presence Activism and Climate Activism

29 Gaby Flores "Meet 12 climate activists changing the world," *Greenpeace International,* December 9, 2021, https://www.greenpeace.org/international/story/51612/meet-12-climate-activists-changing-world/.

30 Tess Lowery, "20 Climate Activists & Organizations to Watch at COP27," *Global Citizen,* November 11, 2022, https://www.globalcitizen.org/en/content/climate-activists-cop27-UN-climate-summit/.

31 *End Fossil: Occupy!,* accessed June 2, 2023, https://endfossil.com/://endfossil.com.

32 *Students Organising for Sustainability,* accessed April 119, 2023, https://www.sos-uk.org/.

33 *SDGTeaching,* accessed April 19, 2023, https://www.sos-uk.org/project/global-goals-teach-in.

34 *The Red Rebel Brigade,* accessed May 24, 2023, http://redrebelbrigade.com/.

35 Andreas Malm, "The moral case for destroying fossil fuel infrastructure," *Guardian,* accessed April 19, 2023, https://www.theguardian.com/commentisfree/2021/nov/18/moral-case-destroying-fossil-fuel-infrastructure?CMP=Share_iOSApp_Other.

36 George Monbiot, "I back saboteurs who have acted with courage and coherence, but I won't blow up a pipeline.

Here's why," *Guardian,* accessed April 19, 2023, https://www. theguardian.com/commentisfree/2023/apr/28/saboteurs-how-to-blow-up-a-pipeline-climate-crisis-direct-action.

37 *Andrew Harvey Institute of Sacred Activism,* online, accessed April 19, 2023, https://www.andrewharvey.net/.

38 Brian Draper, "Talking the Walk, an Interview with Satish Kumar," *High Profiles,* September 3, 2013, https://highprofiles. info/interview/satish-kumar/.

39 Starhawk, *Reclaiming Movement,* online, accessed April 19, 2023, https://starhawk.org/.)

Chapter 6 Embodying Presence Activism in the World

40 "16 ways to take action on climate," *United Nations environmental programme,* online, accessed April 19, 2023, https://www.unep.org/news-and-stories/story/16-ways-take-action-climate.

41 Bill McKibben, founder of 350.org, online, accessed April 19, 2023, 350.org.

42 Caroline Lucas "Radical local policies can build the Green New Deal. Why communities are vital to tackling the multiple crises we face," *New Statesman,* online, March 1, 2023, https://www. newstatesman.com/spotlight/regional-development/2023/03/ radical-local-policies-tackle-multiple-crises.

43 *Glastonbury Town Deal,* online, accessed April 19, 2023, https://glastonburytowndeal.co.uk/.

44 *Faith in Nature website,* online, accessed April 19, 2023, https:// www.faithinnature.co.uk/pages/avotefornature.

Chapter 7 Presence Flower Illuminations

45 Hameed Almaas, "Nonduality: The Nondual Nature of Reality (Enlightenment)," *Diamond Approach,* online, February 10, 2023, https://online.diamondapproach.org/ nonduality-the-nondual-nature-of-reality-enlightenment/.

Bibliography

Albrecht, G. *Earth Emotions: New Words for a New World*. New York: Cornell University Press, 2019.

Aldred, K.L. *Mentorship with goddess: growing sacred womanhood*. Norway: Girl God Books, 2022.

Aldred, K. L. and D. Aldred, *Embodied Education, Creating Space for Learning, Facilitating and Sharing*. Norway: Girl God Books, 2023.

Almaas, A.H. *The Void: Inner Spaciousness and Ego Structure*. Boston: Shambhala Publications, 1986.

Almaas, A.H. *Essence with the Elixir of Enlightenment: The Diamond Approach to Inner Realisation*. York Beach: Samuel Weiser Inc, 1986.

Almaas, A.H. *Facets of Unity: The Enneagram of Holy Ideas*. Berkley: Diamond Books, 1990.

Almaas, A. H. *The Inner Journey Home: The Soul's Realization of the Unity of Reality*. Boston: Shambhala, 2004.

Almaas, A.H. *The Unfolding Now: Realizing Your True Nature through the Practice of Presence*. Boston: Shambhala, 2008.

Almaas, A.H. *Runaway Realization: Living a Life of Ceaseless Discovery*. Boston: Shambhala Publications, 2014.

Almaas A.H. *The Alchemy of Freedom: The Philosopher's Stone and the Secrets of Existence*. Boulder: Shambhala, 2017.

Armstrong, K. *Sacred Nature: How We Can Recover Our Bond with the Natural World*. London: Penguin, 2022.

Aspey, L., C. Jackson, and D. Parker editors. *Holding the Hope: Reviving Psychological and Spiritual Agency in the Face of Climate Change*. Monmouth: PCCS Books Ltd., 2023.

Bendell, J. and Rupert Read. editors. *Deep Adaptation: Navigating the Realities of Climate Chaos*. Cambridge: Polity, 2021.

Bendell, J. *Breaking Together: A Freedom-Loving Response to Collapse*. Bristol: Good Works, 2023.

Blaby, A. *Eco-Anxiety: A Mindful Approach to an Uncertain Future.* Self published, 2022.

Blackie, S. *If Women Rose Rooted: A Life-Changing Journey to Authenticity and Belonging.* Tewkesbury: September Publishing, 2016.

Blackie, S. The *Enchanted Life: Unlocking the Magic of the Everyday.* Tewkesbury: September Publishing, 2018.

Bly, R. *A Little Book on the Human Shadow.* New York: Harper Collins, 1988.

Biabani, Z. *Climate Optimism: Climate Wins and Creating Systemic Change around the World.* Miami: Mango, 2023.

Bogard, P. editor. *Solastalgia: An Anthology of Emotion in a Disappearing World.* Charlottesville: University of Virginia Press, 2023.

Brother Lawrence. *The Practice of the Presence of God.* London: Hodder and Stoughton, 1991.

Brown, M. *The Presence Process: A Healing Journey into Present Moment.* Vancouver: Namaste Publishing, 2005.

Catton, W R. *Overshoot: The Ecological Basis of Revolutionary Change.* Illinois: University of Illinois Press, 1982.

Chenoweth, E. and M. J. Stephan *Why Civil Resistance Works: The Strategic Logic of Nonviolent Conflict.* New York: Columbia University Press, 2011.

Craft, B. *Everything That Rises: A Climate Change Memoir,.* Chicago: Chicago Review Press, 2023.

Cuddy, A. *Presence: Bringing Your Boldest Self to Your Biggest Challenges.* London: Orion, 2015.

Dahr, J. *The End of Ice: Bearing Witness and Finding Meaning in the Path of Climate Disruption and the Burning of the Amazon Rainforest.* New York NY: The New Press, 2019.

Dahr, J. "Grieving My Way into Loving the Planet." In *A Wild Love for the World Joanna Macy and the Work of Our Time,* edited by Stephanie Kaza. Boulder: Shambala, 2020.D'Souza, S. and Bui K. *Not Being: The Art of Self-Transformation* London: Lid Publishing Ltd, 2021.

Dyer, H. *Eco-Anxiety and What to Do About It*. London: Vie Books, 2020.

Engler, M. and P. Engler. *This Is an Uprising: how Nonviolent Revolt is Shaping the Twenty First Century*. New York: Nations Books, 2016.

Extinction Rebellion. *This Is Not a Drill: Extinction Rebellion Handbook*. London: Penguin, 2019.

Figueres, C. and T. Rivett-Carnac. *The Future We Choose: Surviving the Climate Crisis*. London: Manila Press, 2020.

Fry, L. and Y. Altman. *Spiritual Leadership in Action: The CEL Story*. Charlotte: IAP Press, 2013.

Gallagher, S. *The Oxford Handbook of the Self*. Oxford: Oxford University Press, 2011.

Garza, A. *The Purpose of Power*. London: Doubleday, 2020.

Gates, B. *How to Avoid a Climate Disaster*. London: Penguin, 2022.

Gennari, A. T. The *Climate Optimist Handbook: How to Shift the Narrative on Climate Change and to Find the Courage to Choose Change*. Lake Placid: Avia Publishing, 2023.

Goodchild, M. "Relational Systems Thinking: That's How Change is Going to Come, From Our Earth Mother." *Journal of Awareness-Based Systems Change* 1, no.1 (2021): 75–103.

Gore, A. *An Inconvenient Truth: The Planetary Emergency of Global Warming and What We Can Do About It*. Pennsylvania: Rodale Press Emmaus, 2006.

Grose, A. *A Guide to Eco-Anxiety: How to Protect the Planet and Your Mental Health*. London: Watkins Publishing, 2020.

Hamilton, C. *Requiem for a Species: Why We Resist the Truth About Climate Change*. New York: Earthscan Publications, 2010.

Harvey, A. *The Hope: A Guide to Sacred Activism*. UK: Hay House Inc, 2009.

Hewlett, S.A. *Executive Presence: The Missing Link between Merit and Success*. New York: Harper Collins, 2014.

hooks b. *All About Love: New Visions*. New York: WmMorrowPB, 2021.

Hutchins, G. *Leading by Nature: The Process of Becoming a Regenerative Leader.* Tunbridge Wells: Wordzworth Publishing, 2022.

Ingram, C. *Passionate Presence Seven Qualities of Awakened Awareness.* London: Element, 2003.

James, W. *The Varieties of Religious Experience: A Study in Human Nature.* London: Penguin, 1982.

Jameson, J. *Leadership in Post-Compulsory Education: Inspiring Leaders of the Future.* UK: David Fulton Publishers, 2005.

Jamil, D. and S. Rushworth, editors. *We Are the Middle of Forever: Indigenous Voices from Turtle Island on the Changing Earth.* New York: The New Press, 2022.

Jones, K. *Priestess of Avalon Priestess of the Goddess: A Renewed Spiritual Path for the 21st Century.* Glastonbury: Ariadne Publications, 2006.

Joseph, M. *Leaders and Spirituality: A Case Study.* Unpublished thesis, Guildford: University of Surrey University, 2002.

Kelsey, E. *Hope Matters: Why Changing the Way We Think is Critical to Solving the Environmental Crisis.* Vancouver: Greystone Books, 2020.

Keltner, D. *Awe: The Transformative Power of Everyday Wonder.* London: Penguin, 2023.

Kendrick, D. *The Climate Is Changing, Why Aren't We?* London: Piatkus, 2020.

Kennedy-Woodard, M. and P. Kennedy-Williams. *Turn the Tide on Climate Anxiety: Sustainable Action for Your Mental Health and the Planet.* London: Jessica Kingsley Publisher 2022.

Kirkeby, O.F. *Management Philosophy: A Radical Normative Perspective.* Berlin: Springer, 2000.

Kolbert, E. *The Sixth Extinction: An Unnatural History.* New York: Henry Holt and Company.

Kolbert, E. *Under a White Sky: The Nature of the Future.* London: The Bodley Head, 2021.

Krauss, L. M. *The Physics of Climate Change.* New York City: Apollo, 2021.

Kumar, S. *Soil, Soul, Society: A New Trinity for Our Time*. London: Leaping Hare Press, 2013.

Landau, I. *Finding Meaning in an Imperfect World*. New York: Oxford University Press, 2020.

Loach, M. *It's Not That Radical: Climate Action to Transform Our World*. London: DK Penguin Random House, 2023.

Lubar, K. and B. L. Halpern. *Leadership Presence: Dramatic Techniques to Reach Out, Motivate, and Inspire*. Sheridan: Gotham Books, 2004.

Ludwig, M. *Together Resilient: Building Community in the Age of Climate Disruption: A Comprehensive Guide to Intentional Communities and Cooperative Living*. USA: Fellowship for Intentional Community, 2017.

Lynas, M. *Our Final Warning: Six Degrees of Climate Emergenc.,* Lisburn: Fourth Estate, 2020.

Macey, J. *Active Hope: How to Face the Mess We're in with Unexpected Resilience and Creative Power*. San Francisco: New World Library, 2022.

Malm, A. *How to Blow Up a Pipeline*. London: Verso, 2021.

Mann, M. *The New Climate War: The Fight to Take Back Our Planet*. UK: Scribe, 2021.

Maslin, M. *How to Save Our Planet: The Facts*. New York: Penguin, 2021.

McKee, K. E. and B. A. Bruce. "Pedagogy: Developing Activist Identities." In *Transformative Leadership in Action Allyship, Advocacy and Activism*, edited by Jacklyn A. Bruce and Katherine E. McKee. Bingley: Emerald Publishing, 2020.

Miller, A., Z. Dutwood, and S. O. Anderson. *Cut Super Climate Pollutants Now!: The Ozone Treaty's Urgent Lessons for Speeding Up Climate Action*. Hampshire: Changemakers, 2021.

Newberg, A. and M. R. Walkman. *How God Changes Your Brain: Breakthrough Findings from a Leading Neuroscientist*. New York: Ballantine Books, 2010

O'Donohue, J. *Benedictus: A Book of Blessings*. London: Bantam Press, 2007.

Pablo, S. and R. Stevens. *How Everything Can Collapse*. Cambridge: Polity, 2020.

Palmer, W. *The Intuitive Body: Discovering the Wisdom of Conscious Embodiment and Aikido*. Berkeley: Blue Snake Books, 2008.

Pine, R. *The Heart Sutra*. New York: Shoemaker and Hoard, 2004.

Porges, S. W. *Polyvagal Safety: Attachment, Communication, Self-Regulation*. New York: WW Norton & Co, 2021.

Ray S. J., *A Field Guide to Climate Anxiety: How to Keep Your Cool on a Warming Planet*. Oakland: University of California Press, 2020.

Read, R. "Riding Two Horses: The Future of Politics and Activism, as We Face Potential Eco-driven Societal Collapse." In *Deep Adaptation, Navigating the Realities of Climate Chaos*, edited by Jem Bendell and Rupert Read, 240-262. Cambridge: Polity, 2021.

Robinson, J. C. *Mystical Activism: Transforming A World In Crisis*. Washington: Changemakers, 2020.

Rodenburg, P. *Presence: How to Use Positive Energy for Success in Every Situation*. London: Penguin, 2007.

Scharmer, C. O. *Theory U: Leading from the Future as It Emerges*. San Francisco USA: Berrett-Koehler, 2009.

Scharmer, C.O. and K. Kaufer. *Leading from the Emerging Future: From Ego-System to Eco-System Economies*. San Francisco: Berrett-Koehler, 2013.

Schwartz, J. *The Neuroscience of Leadership: Harnessing the Brain Gain Advantage*. London: Palgrave Macmillan, 2015.

Scouller, J. *The Three Levels of Leadership: How to Develop Presence, Knowhow and Skill*. Oxford: Management Books, 2011.

Sedgmore, L. *Fostering Innovative Organisational Cultures and High Performance through Explicit Spiritual Leadership*. Unpublished thesis. Winchester: University of Winchester.

Sedgmore, L. *The Goddess Luminary Leadership Wheel: A Post-Patriarchal Paradigm.* Winchester: Changemakers Books, 2021.

Senge, P., C.O. Scharma, J. Jaworski, and B. Flowers. *Presence: Exploring Profound Change in People, Organizations and Society.* London: Nicholas Brealey, 2005.

Shah, A. K. and A. Rankin.*Jainism and Ethical Finance.* UK: Routledge, 2017.

Sharot, T. *The Influential Mind,* London: Abacus, 2018.

Sidents M., E. Thompson and D. Zahavi. editors *Self, No Self?: Perspectives from Analytical, Phenomenological and Indian Traditions.* Oxford: Oxford University Press, 2011.

Silsbee, D. *Presence-Based Coaching.* San Francisco: Jossey-Bass, 2008.

Starhawk. *The Spiral Dance. A rebirth of the Ancient Religion of the Great Goddess.* New York: Harper Collins, 1979.

Starhawk, *The Earth Path: Grounding Your Spirit in the Rhythms of Nature.* New York, HarperOne, 2006.

Stoknes, P. E. *What We Think About When We Try Not to Think About Global Warming.* Vermont: Chelsea Green Publishing, 2015.

Tait, A. "Climate Psychology and It's Relevance to Deep Adaptation." In *Deep Adaptation, Navigating the Realities of Climate Chaos,* edited by Jem Bendell and Rupert Read, 105-122. Cambridge: Polity, 2021.

Taylor, S. *DisConnected: The Roots of Human Cruelty and How Connection Can Heal the World.* Winchester: IFF Books, 2023.

Thunberg G. *The Climate Book.* London: Penguin, 2022.

Tolle, E. *The Power of Now.* London: Hodder and Stoughton, 1999.

Tolle, E. *Practising The Power of Now: A Guide to Spiritual Enlightenment.* London: Hodder and Stoughton, 2002.

Tolle, E. *Stillness Speaks Whispers of Now* London: Hodder and Stoughton, 2003.

Topa, W. (Four Arrows) and D. Navaez. *Restoring the Kinship World View: Indigenous Voices Introduce 28 Precepts for Rebalancing Life on Planet Earth.* Berkeley: North Atlantic Books, 2022.

Van Dernoot Lipsky, L. *The Age of Overwhelm: Strategies for the Long Haul.* San Francisco: Berrett-Koehler Publishers, 2018.

Van Staden, E. *Leading from Within: The Spirituality and Development of the Contemplative Leader.* Unpublished doctoral thesis: Bloemfontein, University of the Free State, 2022.

Wallace-Wells, D. *The Uninhabitable Earth: A Story of the Future.* London: Penguin, 2019.

Wardley, T. *The Eco Hero Handbook: Simple Solutions to Tackle Eco-Anxiety.* Brighton: Ivy Press, 2021.

Way, B. *Generation Dread: Finding Purpose in an Age of Climate Crisis.* Canada: Alfred A. Knopf, 2022.

Western, S. *Leadership: A Critical Text*: CA, Sage Publications Ltd, 2019.

Western, S. and Lynne Sedgmore. "A Privileged Conversation" *Journal of Management Spirituality and Religion* 5, no. 3 (2008): 321–346.

Wheatley, M. *Who Do We Choose to Be? Facing Reality, Claiming Leadership, Restoring Sanity.* San Francisco: Berrett-Koehler, 2017.

White, M. T*he End of Protest: New Playbook for Revolution.* Canada: Alfred A. Knopf, 2016.

White, R. *Climate Change Criminology.* Bristol: Bristol University Press, 2018.

Wilson, E. O. *Biophilia.* Cambridge: Harvard University Press, 1990.

Wright, S. G. *Heartfullness: The Way of Contemplation: 12 Steps to Freedom Awakening and the Beloved.* Penrith: Sacred Space Publications, 2021.

CHANGEMAKERS
BOOKS

Transform your life, transform our world. Changemakers
Books publishes books for people who seek to become
positive, powerful agents of change. These books
inform, inspire, and provide practical wisdom
and skills to empower us to write the next
chapter of humanity's future.

www.changemakers-books.com

Current Bestsellers from Changemakers Books

Resetting our Future: Am I Too Old to Save the Planet?
A Boomer's Guide to Climate Action
Lawrence MacDonald
Why American boomers are uniquely responsible for
the climate crisis — and what to do about it.

Resetting our Future: Feeding Each Other Shaping
Change in Food Systems through Relationship
Michelle Auerbach and Nicole Civita
Our collective survival depends on making food systems
more relational; this guidebook for shaping change in
food systems offers a way to find both security and
pleasure in a more connected, well-nourished life.

Resetting Our Future: Zero Waste Living, The 80/20 Way
The Busy Person's Guide to a Lighter Footprint
Stephanie J. Miller
Empowering the busy individual to do the easy things that
have a real impact on the climate and waste crises.

The Way of the Rabbit
Mark Hawthorne
An immersion in the world of rabbits: their habitats,
evolution and biology; their role in legend, literature,
and popular culture; and their significance
as household companions.